DEADLY GAMBLE

The Wreck of Schooner *Levin J Marvel*

Deadly Gamble

The Wreck of Schooner
Levin J Marvel

The true story of Chesapeake Bay's
worst sailing disaster

By Kathy Bergren Smith

with the photography of
A. Aubrey Bodine

New Bay Books

DEADLY GAMBLE:
The Wreck of Schooner *Levin J Marvel*
The true story of Chesapeake Bay's worst sailing disaster

by Kathy Bergren Smith
With the photography of A. Aubrey Bodine

Editors
Sandra Olivetti Martin
with Felix Tower

New Bay Books
Fairhaven, Maryland
NewBayBooks@gmail.com

Design by Suzanne Shelden
Shelden Studios
Prince Frederick, Maryland
sheldenstudios@comcast.net

Cover Photo:
Levin J Marvel under sail
(Photo by A. Aubrey Bodine. All Bodine photos are courtesy
of AAubreyBodine.com, copyright Jennifer B. Bodine.)

A Note on Type: Cover and section heads are set in Gil Sans.
                   Text font is Garamond Premier Pro

Library of Congress
Cataloging-in-Publication Data
ISBN 979-8-9853477-5-3
Printed in the United States of America
First Edition

DEDICATION

To my friend, Bill Verge,
and my father, John Bergren.
These maritime adventurers taught me
that a good story is in the telling.

Preface

The Lasting Legacy of the Schooner
Levin J Marvel

Along the waterfront in the small village of North Beach, Maryland, there is a broad view across Chesapeake Bay. The Eastern Shore is barely visible on most days. Wind-swept waves crossing the Bay from east to west break on a long rock jetty that protects the promenade and the community.

On August 12, 1955, 14 people lost their lives in these waters as bodies battered on the breakwater meant to offer protection. There is no marker commemorating that day the Bay raged. A few old-timers remember the terrible afternoon when a young woman, staggering in driving rain and tropical storm-force winds, collapsed onto the beach.

She said that the pleasure schooner, *Levin J Marvel*, had broken up and sunk. There were 26 others out there somewhere, fighting for their lives.

The entire village mobilized in an instant. They launched a remarkable effort to save those lives. The heroic rescues of that day have no memorial.

Little is left of that 128-foot sailing ship, which sank just to the north. Its wreckage is scattered along the bottom, barely a blip on a depth recorder.

The drama that unfolded near this small town, however, took more lives than any other maritime disaster in the Maryland waters of the Chesapeake. Its legacy, apart from the lives lost and forever altered, is written larger than a historical marker. It is written into the Federal Register. That shipwreck contributed to passage of legislation protecting passengers on the water.

—Kathy Bergren Smith

TABLE OF CONTENTS

ANNAPOLIS
.. HOME PORT — WHERE THE CRUISE BEGINS AND ENDS

MARYLAND

N
W S E
NOT DRAWN TO SCALE
NOT YET!

THROUGH RECLAIMED YACHT RACE TO ANNAPOLIS

THE MAUD GIVING HER STERN TO A FAST SAILING BUGEYE

SWIMMING HERE
OH, HOW THEY DO STING

.. OXFORD ..
A PRETTY PLACE

.... A FEW HOURS ASHORE ON SOLOMONS ...

WATERMELONS

THE GIRL FROM BOSTON WHOSE ANCESTORS STOOD THEIR GROUND ON BUNKER HILL .....

POTOMAC RIVER

VIRGINIA

YORK RIVER

TANGIER BOMBER

COAST GUARD

CRISFIELD

TAIN'T MANY OF HER KIND STILL LEFT ON THE BAY!

VISITING ON TANGIER ISLAND
A QUAINT PLACE ...

THE EASTERN SHO'

SIGHT-SEEING IN .. WILLIAMSBURG ..
WHERE COLONIAL ATMOSPHERE HAS BEEN RESTORED ...

SAILING BY NIGHT TO TANGIER

INFERNAL FEMALE CHATTER

FREDDIE THE MATE

OUR GEORGE

THE BELL-BUOYS WINK AND TOLL THEIR MOURNFUL TUNE ....

.. YORKTOWN ..
A VISIT TO THE SPOT WHERE WASHINGTON WHIPPED THE BRITISH UNDER CORNWALLIS

GIRLS!

BALTIMORE

JAMES RIVER

.. NORFOLK ..

The CRUISE of the
Edwin and Maud

STEES

Part Three: THE TRIAL

Introduction

August 12, 1955

Hurricane Connie wobbled like a drunken pirate toward the mid-Atlantic coast of the U.S. in early August 1955. In the late hours of August 11, Connie turned inland and began tracking a course up Chesapeake Bay. Here, the storm turned its fury on a three-masted schooner, *Levin J Marvel*, with 27 people on board, attempting to return to Annapolis, Maryland, after a pleasure cruise on the Bay.

By dawn, Connie's outermost bands reached *Marvel*. These were gusty northeast winds, challenging the canvas on the 64-year-old ship. The wind's intensity steadily increased. A 40-to-50-mile-an-hour gust tore away *Marvel's* mainsail. It flapped and threatened to fly overboard, creating drag and mayhem. The captain called into the dining salon to breakfasting passengers to help with the sails. They struggled to lower the great foresail, leaving just one sail and a small staysail to help steer the ship. There was no motor to assist. The schooner ran before the wind across the Chesapeake. By 8am, the wind and rain had whipped up a mist engulfing *Marvel* in whiteness.

The captain's best hope was to make for the shelter of the exposed shore and anchor before the ship was smashed. Passengers breathed a sigh of relief and had a light lunch. Then, things went downhill fast.

A young deckhand watched in horror as a 500-gallon water tank, bolted on deck midships, tore free and hurtled to the stern. The huge projectile tore off a hatch cover and headed for the lounge, where the passengers were gathered. It glanced off the corner of the deckhouse, broke the railing and went overboard.

Large waves broke across the deck, pouring water down from above while bursting through portholes. Securing the portholes was impossible. Some had missing wingnuts, and some were stuck. Water was rising so quickly in the cabins that pumps could not keep up with the flooding. To staunch the flow, passengers frantically stuffed blankets into the ports while standing thigh-deep in water.

As the anchor dragged, another was tossed over in the hope of securing the ship and buying time. But there was no time left for *Marvel*. The ship began to pull apart as wave after wave pounded on her timbers.

Survival now meant abandoning ship. The captain began passing a line through the lifejacket straps of one then another passenger, in hopes of keeping the group together.

Hours earlier, there had been a sense of exhilaration as *Marvel* plowed quickly through the rain and whipping waves, presumably headed for safety.

Now the terrified group made for the deck and the unknown. The same question on each of their minds: "Will we make it out alive?"

The "LEVIN J. MARVEL"

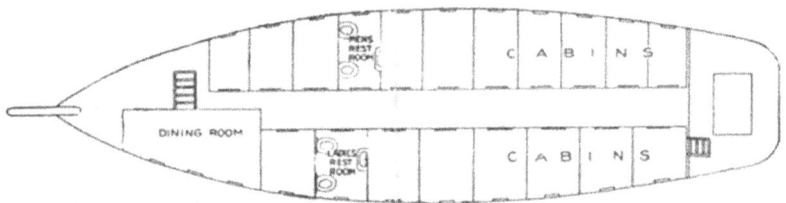

Part I

from
RAM SCHOONER
to
DUDE CRUISER

Chapter One

Take a "Dude Cruise" on a Chesapeake Windjammer

Levin J Marvel sank on August 12, 1955, abandoning 27 people to the wind and the waves. By this time, the old ship had sailed thousands and thousands of miles and been abandoned twice itself. *Marvel* was built in 1891, when the best and most efficient way to move cargo like lumber and fertilizer up and down the East Coast was under sail. The winds shifted in the 1930s, when trucks and small motorized vessels took over the cargo trade. Sailing on the Chesapeake was turned over to yachtsmen and watermen. One after another, the old schooners sailed off to shipyards in Norfolk, Virginia or Baltimore to undergo the disfiguring operation "demasting and repowering," that is, having their masts severed and World War II surplus diesel engines installed. Many were just left to languish.

That first generation of motorized freight-hauling vessels on the Chesapeake was utilitarian. There was little beauty in the loud chugging diesel or coal-fired engines. Cargo-carrying sailing ships became rarer, taking on a new role in the imagination: a romantic vision of a bygone era. It took Herman Knust, a visionary outsider, to conceive of a new career for old *Levin J Marvel.*

Herman Knust with his two-ship windjammer fleet c.1950

Knust was born in Canada in 1892. His family moved to Maryland shortly after his birth and settled on a farm in Howard County. Like many farm boys, Knust had early exposure and an affinity for mechanics, but he also heard the call of the wild.

At 13, Knust ran away from home and worked dredging oysters through a Potomac winter. His family blamed that episode on a book he was reading at the time about a boy "running away to sea." At 24, he joined General Pershing's Maryland Militia and chased Poncho Villa through the Mexican desert.

After several years of adventuring, he settled into a practical career making things work. He learned black-smithing, then used his skill in manipulating heavy metals as a mechanic with the railroad. He ran the Mount Clare repair and maintenance facility for the B&O Railroad and was promoted to division superintendent.

Approaching 50, Knust was ready for a new challenge. He took a year's leave of absence from the railroad. During this break, he adopted the idea of the "dude cruise," modeled on the popular windjammer cruises in Maine that gave landlubbers a taste of what life aboard a sailing ship might have been like, but with enough creature comforts and good food to be a vacation. He found the languishing 128-foot cargo schooner *Levin J Marvel* and bought her for $2,000. *Marvel's* design was well-suited to his idea. She was a "ram" schooner, a nearly flat-bottomed ship that had plenty of space below decks.

He rebuilt the ship to the specifications of his imagination. The vast empty cargo hold was divided into 17 small staterooms, each with a porthole and a brass sink, for the guests he hoped would come. He created a large lounge in a deckhouse on the stern. He added a dining salon in the bow with a galley above. In the transformed *Levin J Marvel*, he had a perfect mix of authentic working ship and cruiser.

Eastern Shore "old salts," who had sailed the ships in their cargo-carrier days, captained the new *Levin J Marvel*, sailing out of Baltimore, starting in June of 1946. The first seasons were completely booked. Riding a wave of enthusiasm, Knust bought *Edwin and Maud,* a ram schooner built in 1900, a near sistership to *Marvel*. Each carried about 30 passengers. With his increasing success, Knust and his ships moved out of the congested Patapsco River to the colonial capital of Maryland, Annapolis. They were an impressive sight at the City Dock. He opened his office at 229 Prince George Street.

The cruises were a counterpoint to the increasingly hectic post-war lives of the urbanites to whom Knust marketed the trips. *Marvel* toured the historic ports in the middle Chesapeake while *Edwin and Maud* embarked on two-week voyages down the Bay to remote Tangier Island and historic towns like Williamsburg and Jamestown. The slow ships gave passengers ample time to relax and unwind on the water. *Edwin and Maud's* crew even included a hostess. She entertained passengers by giving sketching lessons and suggesting excursions for port calls.

Here's a . .

"Different Vacation"

Cruising the *Historic* Chesapeake Bay

A Voyage To Remember

Aboard the Levin J. Marvel

CHESAPEAKE'S WINDJAMMER VACATION ANNAPOLIS, MD.

Souvenir postcard

The cruises were fun. They were a vacation opportunity for families before the era of theme parks. For young singles, they were an adventure and a chance to enjoy the company of strangers. Both ships regularly sold out.

Nearing 60, Knust was again ready for something new. After the summer of 1952, he bought a farm in rural Virginia. He closed the office on Prince George Street in Annapolis and took no reservations for the following summer. The better of the two ships, *Edwin and Maud,* moved to Maine, with Frederick Guild continuing the business in Penobscot Bay, where Knust had gotten this idea from windjammer cruises. Tied up in Salisbury at its winter berth, *Levin J Marvel* again languished as if waiting for another dreamer to come along.

John Meckling was that dreamer. He was 37, a tall, handsome, likable Pennsylvanian with twinkling blue eyes. Meckling, like Knust, was a restless man. But unlike Knust, who seemed to create success with his every move, Meckling had not quite found his niche. He had served in the Coast Guard during World War II but was too much of a free spirit to remain content within the bureaucracy of the military. He had the busy mind of a tinkerer—he was an avid reader of *Popular Mechanics*—always deconstructing and reassembling.

After the war, he skipped the free education offered by the GI Bill to throw himself into auto racing. With ever-increasing breath-taking speed, the sport captured post-war American imagination. Meckling lived with his wife in Central Pennsylvania and was a regular on the stock car racetracks there. His automotive expertise translated into a short-lived career as a Ford salesman. Then he began an ill-fated business selling transmission equipment for televisions. His heart was just not in it.

For all his fascination with speed and modern technology from cars to televisions, he long was driven to return to the waterfront. He had been bitten hard by the sailing bug when he was a teen visiting the Great

Lakes. Before he married, he had made frequent visits to the Chesapeake and bought a skipjack from a Deal Island waterman on the far reaches of the Eastern Shore. The skipjack was the ubiquitous workboat oystermen used throughout the region. Meckling explored the Bay, sailing his boat to the small fishing ports of St. Michaels and Oxford, foreshadowing trips he would later take.

John Meckling took a sail with Herman Knust aboard *Levin J Marvel* in 1952, and when he learned that the ship was laid up, he went straight to Salisbury to have a look. He saw the masts of *Levin J Marvel* stretching up 90 feet, tipped with white paint, the golden pine spars towering above the surrounding workboats in the marina on the Wicomico River. The ship was like a lost visitor from a different century. Meckling immediately wanted to sail this ship.

Herman Knust met with Meckling and liked him, just as most anyone who met him. Knust thought he had the right combination of charisma and competence to carry on "dude cruising" on the Chesapeake. Meckling, himself, was very keen to pick up the business. But he had little in the way of capital or borrowing ability, so the sale was mothballed—along with *Marvel*.

CHAPTER TWO

Striking the Sails:
A Brief History of the End
of Schooner Trade on the Bay

It was not at all uncommon to see vessels like *Marvel* laid up or abandoned in the 1950s. Most of the cargo-carrying sailing ships were long gone by then. Highways and trucking were evolving, and goods moved faster on the roadway or railroad. But during the heyday of coastal water transport, the ram schooner had been a successful class of ship.

This unique schooner was designed by JMC Moore shipbuilders in Bethel, Delaware in the 1880s. Created to be a competitive freight hauler to run in a specific area, it was not designed to go out onto the high seas. Its home was the inland waters along the East Coast. Mainly, though, it was designed to navigate the narrow canal connecting the Chesapeake and Delaware bays.

That canal, which opened in 1829, was a link for both north- and south-bound marine traffic. A ship traveling between Baltimore and Philadelphia by canal could shave off 300 miles and a week or more from its voyage. Before the canal, getting from Baltimore and Philadelphia required sailing the length of the Chesapeake south to Norfolk, Virginia and out into the Atlantic, then up the coast to the entrance to the Delaware Bay near Cape

May, New Jersey. The original canal, 10 feet deep and only 68 feet wide, had three locks. The federal government purchased the canal in 1919 and began plans to expand it and remove the locks. Subsequent expansions have kept the canal open and passable for tug and barge as well as ship traffic.

The old locks determined the parameters the Bethel yards used to build the fleet. The typical ram was in the neighborhood of 130 feet long with a 28-foot beam. This narrow beam still only gave the ships a few inches on either side while locking through the old canal. Another design parameter was the draft of these vessels. With a centerboard that let the draft remain under 10 feet, the boats worked the shallow tributaries of the Tidewater region. A deep-draft keelboat would never make it into these tiny ports.

The name "ram" is most likely a reference to the brawniness of the design. If sailing cargo ships were the trucks of the Chesapeake and Great Lakes, the ram schooners were the tandem tractor trailers. They were engaged in bulk cargo trade, specifically, shipping lumber from the Carolinas north to the building-boom cities in the Northeast. The ships then filled their holds with fertilizer from the factories in Baltimore and coal from Appalachia to deliver to the farms of Virginia and the Carolinas.

The ships were three-masted. Built for strength, not speed, they did not carry the multiple sails above their mainsails or multiple foresails of the great clipper ships. The standard sail set on a ram was a jib and a staysail flying before the foremast. Three masts of equal height carried a foresail, a mainsail and a mizzen, often called a "spanker." Fewer sails also left a lot more room on deck since there was no standing rigging to haul those topsails. The open deck space was available, then, to load more lumber than would fit in the holds. The deck cargo was known to be the "crew's take." These were off-the-books deals that the crew made at the dock. They loaded the extra lumber on deck and then sold it for their own profit.

There was one small gasoline engine onboard, but it was not for propulsion. The engine, called a "donkey," was used to turn a rotating cylinder, called a capstan. A single deckhand could take a couple of turns of line around the slowly rotating capstan and let the engine do the work of hauling the heavy canvas sails up the masts. The donkey made it possible to sail the ship with a skeleton crew, making it more economical. When hauling cargo, the rams could be operated by the captain and two deckhands. There was no engine below decks. The schooners relied upon a small following motor launch, called a "yawl boat," to push the ship in tight quarters or when the wind died. The yawl boat would be towed behind or hung on davits to keep it close at hand.

By the 1940s even the rams, with their specialized clientele and ability to carry heavy loads, were becoming obsolete. There were fewer and fewer in service each year. The summer of 1955, when *Levin J Marvel* sank, a second ram also was lost. A ship very similar to *Marvel*, *Edward R Baird Jr.*—which had survived an attack by a German U-boat on June 4, 1918—nearly sank off the coast of

Virginia. The 1918 attack was one of many that the early submarines made on merchant ships. The crew was picked up by a US Navy ship, and the *Baird* was towed to Norfolk, where it returned to service in the fleet of the Worcester Fertilizer Company.

The *Baird's* renewed career ended after her last captain died. She was laid up and abandoned, another relic. But this ram schooner had one more voyage to take. She was resurrected by Charles Staples, a 30-year-old chemical engineer with DuPont looking for a new start. Like Meckling, he had the ability to imagine the ship back at work. The ship was an impressive size, and Staples later told a newspaper reporter that "there is good money hauling certain cargoes." His plan was to return her to cargo hauling.

The new owner allocated $30,000 to the project, paying the first $2,000 to take the vessel off the hands of the Worcester Fertilizer Company. Then Staples did what he could to make the vessel safe for a trip to Baltimore for drydocking. He made simple repairs to the topsides plus some manner of recaulking to areas that had dried up. While there was logic to his plan, its execution was casual.

For the trip to the shipyard, Staples gathered his crew, but not from the legions of watermen in the area. Instead, he took his mother as cook and hired three Midwestern university students who hoped to work the ship for a share of profits. Two art students and a journalism major, they were looking for inspiration. Presumably, they were hoping to capture Age of Sail imagery. Just like Meckling, they encountered the wind field of an approaching hurricane. This one was named Ione.

It had only been a month since the sister ship *Marvel* sank amid tropical storm-force winds. Surely, Staples was aware of the tragedy and the Coast Guard investigation just getting underway. Even so, the voyage went on as planned. The captain freely admitted later that he had not checked the weather forecast before setting off for a picnic outing on September 12. Storm warnings were flying that day on the Tangier Sound when he sailed from Crisfield.

The ship's true condition soon made itself clear in the short, steep seas of the shallows. While attempting to pull in the yawl boat, the crew lost both the boat and the young man running it. The captain radioed the Coast Guard, who quickly sent a response boat. The crewman on the yawl boat was picked up and the other passengers and the captain were rescued. The only casualty of this voyage was the ship itself. The old U-boat survivor sank as it was towed toward shore.

The *Baird* did inspire art, though not by its student crew. The Baltimore-based photographer Aubrey Bodine captured the ship as it sat on the bottom in a well-known image, "Cradle of the Deep."

Marvel's closer sistership had a much luckier fate than either her or the *Baird*. In 1900, JMC Moore shipyard launched *Edwin and Maud,* built for the same owner as *Marvel.* The younger ship was named for the captain's little children, who were less a part of his life than their namesake. In near-constant trade, the busy rams gave

their captains and crew few opportunities to return home to Delaware.

Forty-six years later, Herman Knust bought *Edwin and Maud* and converted it to passenger service, first hauling the boat and completely refurbishing it.

Edwin and Maud continued her working life in Maine after Knust closed his Chesapeake business, joining a windjammer syndicate as one of the largest ships in the fleet.. She was renamed *Victory Chimes* in homage to World War I victory celebrations. Unlike *Marvel*, *Victory Chimes* never fell into serious disrepair. She has sailed almost continuously for over 120 years, and still sails Downeast Maine cruises.

Jennie D Bell was the last of the rams to work on the Chesapeake. Clarence Heath was captain and part owner of the ship for some 50 years and owner-operator for most of that time. His skill as a captain was renowned: It is said that the ship was grounded only twice in its long career under Captain Heath.

Heath and his wife, Mamie, made their home in Seaford, Delaware, where they raised three sons. As *Jennie D Bell* and her captain grew older and the children went off on their own, Mrs. Heath joined her husband, living aboard *Jennie D Bell* with their seven dogs as the old ship made its rounds hauling grain from the small ports of the Tidewater region to Salisbury, Maryland.

The elderly Heaths' floating home had the distinction of being not only the last of the ram schooners working on the Bay but also the largest sailing vessel registered as an active freight-hauling ship in the United States Merchant

Marine Registry. Ultimately, a very difficult winter in 1961 cost the *Bell* two large sails. That loss coupled with a dockworker strike to persuade the Heaths to move ashore. They hoped to sell the ship into the passenger trade, but there were no buyers. *Jennie D Bell* was beached on a shallow bar in the Wicomico River, standing sentinel as she slowly rotted.

A. Aubre. ?

Third Chance for
Levin J Marvel

The tide turned for the *Levin J Marvel* early in the summer of 1954. Step by step, John Meckling was getting the sailing ship back in action. By mid-June, his financing was nailed down. John Evans, a Pennsylvania acquaintance, agreed to be a silent partner in the enterprise, giving full control of the operation to Meckling. Herman Knust sold *Marvel*, the business name and the old advertising brochures to the partnership for $7,500.

The ship was in rough shape. Even a do-it-yourselfer like Meckling knew it needed more help than he could swing with the money he had on hand. He spent an additional $7,000 on new rigging and a 25-foot yawl boat. The ship also needed new floorboards and mattresses for the cabins because the old had been ruined by water that had crept into the hull while the ship was mothballed. Meckling hired local carpenters to make repairs and put a fresh coat of paint in dank areas below the deck.

Neither had the old white hull weathered well in a year in the weeds. Enough money was on hand to have *Marvel* painted where it showed: above the waterline. But there was no money to haul the boat and refurbish it, as had been done to *Edwin and Maud, Marvel's* sister ship

Now, the ship needed to be generating income. With work underway, Chesapeake Windjammer Cruises advertised cruises starting in late July and continuing through October. He was as ready as he could afford to go to sea.

Levin J Marvel underway c. 1950

Meckling hoped to cash in, as Knust had, by marketing to the city-dwellers looking for a unique summertime escape. Repeating Knust's strategy, he placed ads in the Washington, Philadelphia and New York Sunday papers. Deposits for weeklong trips at $85 per person began trickling in.

The next step was to organize a berth for the enormous ship. Meckling arranged with the Annapolis harbormaster to put *Marvel* at the end of the City Dock, a high visibility spot where it had spent prior seasons.

The position offered easy access to the Severn River and out to the Bay.

To support Meckling's sailing dreams, the family had moved to Annapolis. Euretta, an easy-going woman, was indulgent of her husband's schemes and happy to play a supporting role to his big personality. She would care for their son, Wayne, and run the business office for Chesapeake Windjammer Cruises from Church Circle, in the center of Annapolis. Euretta found a small boarding house where she and Wayne could stay during the season. In winter, the family planned to live aboard to save on lodging. The project seemed to be falling into place.

To learn to sail his ship, Meckling reached out to Bill Tawes, who had skippered both *Marvel* and its sistership, *Edwin and Maud*, under Knust. A Salisbury native, Tawes knew the winding Wicomico River and the Chesapeake from Norfolk to Delaware. The men would sail together to Annapolis from Salisbury on a familiarization cruise.

With the clock ticking, pressure was high. The first passengers were scheduled to board *Marvel* on Monday, July 19. The new rigging was finally installed and tuned, and the ship was ready to go on July 15. Another Salisbury native signed on as cabin boy. Bill Hall, a 16-year-old rising high school senior, brought his sea bag, intending on staying aboard the ship through the summer. As the ship sailed from Salisbury, two local carpenters were also onboard, finishing the interior work on the water-damaged cabins.

Flush with confidence, Meckling brought his six-year-old son, Wayne, on the trip, along with the family's two pet parakeets.

Marvel sailed on the ebb tide close to midnight on July 15. Underway at last, Meckling failed to see the reality of his situation. After two years out of the water, *Marvel's* problems went beyond what some paint and carpentry could solve. A wooden ship must be kept in the water to remain afloat. Otherwise, the planking dries out, shrinks and pulls away from the heavy timbers that form its frame. The tarred fibrous oakum used to caulk the seams dries and disintegrates over time. Once a ship returns to the water, it takes some time for the planks to swell and reseal the seams. If it has been left too long, it will not reseal adequately; the ship will leak.

When *Marvel* left Salisbury, Captain Tawes soon felt the stern of the old ship "settling" or sinking. The failing seams in the stern were flooding the bilge with water. Two gasoline-powered bilge pumps were not enough to keep up with the inflow. About eight and a half miles below Salisbury, Captain Tawes had no choice but to drive the ship onto a mudbank. It was going to sink.

The City of Salisbury's fire boat, *Frederick A Grier,* came to the aid of the stranded schooner. Captain Dana Richard and his six-man crew arrived on the scene around 10:30am July 16 and pumped for four hours. The water continued to pour in; even the fireboat's pumps were not enough to keep up. The situation became more dire, for as the tide rose the ship began to sink all over again. Captain Richards called the Coast Guard, and in the late afternoon a cutter arrived from Crisfield, Maryland, perhaps that same one that would assist the *Edward R Baird* the following summer. It took several more hours of pumping by both the cutter and the fireboat for the ship to be refloated. A local waterman, Corrie Dickerson, towed *Marvel* to a boatyard in the nearby town of Whitehaven.

Ever the optimist, Meckling seemed unperturbed by the near sinking of his new business. He told the local paper that "all she needs is a good caulking, and that will cost me $50." But the delay would cost him more than that. One by one, he lost his entourage. Euretta picked up Wayne, the parakeets had long since flown the coop, the cabin boy decided to find other employment and Captain Tawes refused to continue the trip. Another blow struck when Brown's Marine Railway at White Haven had no opening for *Marvel*.

Meckling was alone on his ship now, save for a man who was hired on as a steward. So virtually singlehanded and with only the most rudimentary knowledge of how to sail *Marvel*, Meckling decided to make the over-100-mile trip to Baltimore. There, at Booz Brothers, a much larger facility than the tiny Eastern Shore boatyards, *Marvel* could be quickly caulked.

A tugboat bound for Baltimore without a tow appeared almost miraculously on the scene. The tug would be going right by Booz Brothers and could get *Marvel* there quickly. In yet another defeat for Meckling, the tug's captain declined to tow the leaky vessel. Meckling decided to make the trip up the Bay himself, pushing the ship with the 25-foot yawl boat.

The *Baltimore Sun* reported on *Marvel's* "hard luck" maiden voyage after picking up the story from the Coast Guard's report in Salisbury. Following Meckling as he headed off for Baltimore, the paper reported, erroneously, that *Marvel* had gone missing around the newly built Chesapeake Bay Bridge near Annapolis. In reality, *Marvel*, like any ram schooner, was very slow, making three to five knots on a good day as Meckling pushed up the Bay.

When Meckling arrived at Booz Brothers Shipyard, on July 22, he was in a hurry. He needed to get to City Dock in Annapolis to begin the season. Already, Meckling was behind schedule, his first cruise canceled and angry ticket holders mollified. He ordered caulking and replacement of rotted planking below the waterline for now. Further work could wait for the off-season.

Running Afoul of the Coast Guard

While in Baltimore, Meckling and *Marvel* had come on the Coast Guard's radar. Meckling would prevail after their first scrimmage, but in so doing he created an enemy more dangerous than he could imagine. Here's how that scrimmage played out:

Meckling's work order had been completed and he was about to sail when Coast Guard marine inspectors arrived unannounced with a notice from the Captain of the Port, Alfred Kabernagel, that the vessel was not to leave without a full inspection. Meckling was caught off guard. Knust had given him no warning of inspections. It was already July 30. His second cruise was scheduled to start, and his money had run out. There was no room for further delay.

Meckling demanded to see Captain Kabernagel, who was the highest-ranking Coast Guard officer in Baltimore. His meeting was acrimonious. Meckling argued, correctly, that the Coast Guard had no jurisdiction over *Marvel*, now a passenger cruiser. Ending the discussion by calling the Captain of the Port of Baltimore a "bastard" and vowing to appeal any further orders to Coast Guard headquarters, Meckling made a powerful enemy.

As problematic as the boat was its unlicensed captain. Insubordinate, inexperienced and confident, Meckling had commented lightheartedly to a Salisbury reporter that he couldn't swim. Kabernagel knew the type, and they were trouble. The idea that Meckling would take passengers for hire on a vessel in such disrepair as *Marvel* was galling to this stout, serious and by-the-book officer.

Meckling was right, though, that *Marvel*, a sailing vessel that was officially documented at 183 gross tons, was far below the threshold of 700-gross tons that triggered inspection requirements for carrying passengers "for hire," in other words, paying customers. As long as it operated strictly as a sailboat, there was not a thing Kabernagel could do about it. Nothing, that is, as long as the yawl did not assist the ship while passengers were aboard. Its assistance would make *Marvel* a powerboat and subject to the rules in place for them. Only when the wind was just right would *Marvel* be able to hoist a sail to get in or out of the Annapolis busy harbor. The yawl boat was a necessity.

Meckling devised a devious plan. Euretta would join the passengers aboard on Monday morning. The yawl would push *Marvel* off the dock. Then, once under sail, she would collect the passengers' money. Thus there were no "paying passengers" aboard when the motor skiff was propelling the ship. Euretta would then daringly jump into the yawl boat, wave goodbye and depart, with a deckhand driving, for the dock. The ruse was essential in the busy Annapolis harbor, with a Coast Guard station nearby. During the cruises, *Marvel* would anchor most nights in the open waters. It would be simple enough, Meckling reasoned, to sail on and off the few piers they visited.

Meckling was sailing through a loophole. Alfred Kabernagel had his eyes on *Marvel*, just waiting to close that loophole—against Meckling and all his ilk.

CHAPTER FOUR

Bringing Order to the Water by Legislating Boating Safety

The very notion of setting sail implies escape. Getting out on the water is a break from the routines and habits of daily life. That was the marketing message of Chesapeake Windjammer Vacations.

In the early 1950s, the near-coastal waters—where people live, make their livings and recreate on the bays, lakes and sounds—were getting crowded thanks to a boom in pleasure boating.

The task of bringing order to the water fell to the Coast Guard. Organized in 1780, before the Navy, the United States Coast Guard was initially a revenue collector, but it quickly morphed into protector. During both world wars, the Coast Guard patrolled the coastal waters, protecting the shores from German U-boats. In peacetime, the role focused on protecting people on these waters. They were the safety monitors. A call for help brought the Coast Guard to the rescue, no matter the weather or the circumstances.

Yet as a branch of the military, the 20th century Coast Guard represented a cultural threat to those they were protecting on the East Coast. Those local mariners—the Maine lobstermen, the Long Island baymen, the Chesapeake watermen—were generation-ally conditioned to figuring things out for themselves.

These are people who don't like being told what to do, especially when it comes to their boats and their activities on the water. They'd have preferred the Coast Guard keep their distance. However, the recreational boating boom was causing chaos in their workplace.

After World War II, the new middle class took to the water in droves. GI's returning home found the water a new place to play. Small motorboats and sailboats appeared in the near coastal waterways that were once the domain of the working mariner or the wealthy yachtsmen. Outboard motor technology advanced, and fiberglass became an affordable hull material.

The boating boom of the 1950s has never been surpassed. *Boating Industry Magazine* reported a total of 450,000 recreational boats registered with the Coast Guard in 1950. By the end of the decade, that number of new boats was registered every year. Brands like Evinrude and Chris-Craft became household names. Boat shows introduced new models of production boats, now manufactured like cars, on the assembly line. In 1954, Chris-Craft had 139 models of its runabouts. Evinrude employed 9000 workers making outboard motors with ever-increasing horsepower.

Even without a boat, people could still get on the water by purchasing a ticket on someone else's vessel. Waterways were suddenly busy with water-skiers, fishermen, cruisers and swimmers, all vying for space with the commercial traffic. With little regulation, inevitably, accidents increased.

Pleasure boating was an entirely unregulated seascape until the late 1950s. Captain Kabernagel, Meckling's newly sworn enemy, had served for twenty-five years as the Chief of Marine Inspections in Baltimore. Investigating marine casualties and preventing them from happening again was his business. He had seen vessels of all sorts wrecked, swamped, sunken and stricken. He had investigated injuries and deaths associated with the accidents. He saw *Levin J Marvel* as not only a danger but also an opportunity.

The Coast Guard had long lobbied Congress to enact legislation regulating passenger and recreational boating industries. *Marvel* and its insouciant captain captured Kabernagel's attention. It took the sinking of two charter boats in Long Island Sound in 1951 to capture attention on the Hill.

Disaster

Each summer, starting in 1932, the Long Island Railroad ran a special weekend excursion trip from New York City to Montauk, on the far end of Long Island. The "Fisherman Special" roundtrip fare was $1.50. People loaded their fishing rods and tackle boxes on the train early in the morning to arrive at Montauk's fishing docks for a 7:30am departure. The fishing boats sold tickets to as many passengers as they could to fish for porgies near the lighthouse. Then the boat returned to the dock and the tired fishermen slept their way back to the city for a fish dinner.

As with *Marvel*, the Coast Guard had no jurisdiction over these small passenger-carrying vessels. They carried as many people as would fit aboard. There was no licensing requirement for the captains, and the boats were not subject to any inspection.

On September 1, 1951, the Fisherman Special was particularly crowded. It was a beautiful morning in the waning days of summer. Captain Eddie Carroll's *Pelican* was late getting underway that day, and the last of the fishermen crowded onto the 47-foot boat. Carroll took 67 passengers aboard for the voyage.

The beautiful morning turned rough as a northeast wind built steadily. *Pelican* joined the rest of the fleet in an area locally called "Frisbees," to fish for the morning. Having gotten off late, *Pelican* stayed out perhaps a bit longer to give passengers a chance to catch a few more fish. The ebbing tide met the wind, creating a steep chop. Waves began to break across the deck, and the panicked passengers rushed to the other side of the vessel, shifting the balance of the overcrowded boat. *Pelican* quickly lost stability and capsized. Other boats rushed to assist and pick up passengers, who were flung into the water with no lifejackets. Yet 47 people drowned that day, including the captain. Coast Guard responded, attempting unsuccessfully to tow *Pelican* to shore. *Pelican*, and the bodies of many passengers, remained out of the harbor until the next day.

This tragedy occurred on the heels of the sinking of a smaller charter boat, the 33-foot *Jack*, earlier that summer. *Jack* was in Gardiner's Bay off Long Island when it ran into trouble. In this case, it was the boat, not the people who caused the sinking. A 50-year old trawler that had undergone demasting repowering, the boat had been hauled the previous July 1950 but was still leaky when Captain Robert Thornton set out on June 10, 1951 with 15 on board.

Small craft warnings were flying as they left Niantic, Connecticut for a day of fishing. The weather got worse and worse, and the fish were not biting. After taking the party to several fishing holes, Thornton gave up and headed home around two in the afternoon. Shortly after the decision to go in, a passenger alerted Thornton to water in the cabin. Within 15 minutes, the *Jack* was completely under water. The old planks had simply dropped away, leaving a huge hole in the hull in the bow. There was no radio to call for help and no life raft. The passengers barely had time to get life preservers from the cabin before going into the water. Eleven died that day. The captain was picked up by another fishing boat, but that boat had trouble and anchored overnight in the weather before Coast Guard came to the rescue.

These and other high-profile accidents were covered in the metropolitan press in New York and Boston, catching the attention of lawmakers. Eventually, Congress would heed the Coast Guard's call for governance over both the passenger boat industry, which included charter or "head" boats, and recreational boating.

It would take five more years for the legislation to reach the desk of President Dwight D. Eisenhower. Along the way, the scant regulation of vessels taking passengers for hire continued, allowing John Meckling to start his first season with little or no regulatory oversight.

CHAPTER FIVE

Reasonable Risk:
Seven Successful Cruises

Chesapeake Bay is a forgiving estuary. Unlike other scenic coastlines, it is not rocky or especially deep or prone to severe tides or currents. Its width in the mid-section, near Annapolis, is narrow enough to bridge. Yet like any estuary—and this is the largest in the world, at 220 miles long—there is the potential for seasonal storms, sudden squalls and the occasional hurricane. That said, there are plenty of places to tuck in to avoid a blow. So Meckling, operating *Marvel* mainly in daylight in the mild summer weather within a small theater of operations, was taking what he saw as a reasonable risk.

The 1954 season, although delayed, was a successful start to the reboot of Chesapeake Windjammer Cruises. Bookings were steady. The early marketing had attracted a well-heeled crowd able and willing to pay $85 for a chance to slow down over a week on the Bay. Always dressed in pressed khakis, Meckling was the epitome of handsome and professional captain as he greeted his guests on Sunday in Annapolis.

The ship had 17 staterooms, each appointed with bunks, a washbasin and a porthole. There were two heads below deck, though one was finicky and couldn't be counted on. There was no permanent shower; sometimes a hose on deck provided a welcome spray down on hot days. The cabins were tight quarters; a tall person would have trouble stretching out on the bunk. Two people and their belongings left no room for lounging. These were sleeping quarters only, and *Marvel* was a social ship. Herman Knust had added a lounge in the stern that served as a common area for passengers. With a radio, the lounge was a comfortable space for spending time and enjoying conversation or listening to music.

Below deck, in the bow, an open dining salon was lined with tables and bench seats. The first family-style meal was usually the icebreaker for the whole trip. A bad joke might be cracked that would then become the inside laugh for the rest of the trip. No matter the group, there was always an almost palpable sense of comradery at the tables. It would be nearly impossible not to interact with your shipmates at mealtimes.

Food was delicious and plentiful. Elroy Pinkney was a memorable character who served as ship's cook. A World War II Navy veteran, Pinkney could prepare Chesapeake specialties while underway that rivaled any seafood eatery. The galley door was always open and "Pinky," as he was called on the ship, was a genial host. He only closed up when he was making his famous crab cakes, as he did on every cruise.

Crab cakes are a regional delicacy in the waters of the Chesapeake and were inexpensive during the crabbing season. Meckling's shoestring operation required Pinky to keep the food service costs low; hence, his penchant for local specialties. Charles Savoy, another Annapolitan, was the good-humored steward who helped keep guests happy. Meckling hired pickup deckhands from the watermen's community who could assist in trimming the sails and tying up the vessel.

ELRY PINKNEY
Ship's Cook Who Survived

CHARLES SAVOY
Rescued Crew Member

Of every cruise, Meckling was the star. After showing the guests their quarters, he invited them to enjoy a wander around downtown Annapolis and told them to make their final stop at Mills Fine Wine and Spirits on City Dock where they could stock up for the voyage.

The sophisticated voyagers were charmed to find Hillard Donner's wine selection rivaled any New York City purveyor's.

On Monday morning, the motorized yawl boat pushed *Marvel* out of the crowded harbor. Meckling gathered the passengers on deck, telling them they were about to embark on a trip back in time. They would be living like the seafarers of 50 years ago. They could assist in the sailing as much or as little as they wished. Their first opportunity was to help hoist the heavy gaff-rigged sails. Invariably, everyone jumped in and began to "Heave! Ho!" When the three enormous sails caught the wind, the rigging groaned as if the history book page had, indeed, been turned to a previous chapter.

Once under sail, Euretta Meckling made the rounds, collecting the passengers' money and issuing receipts. A deckhand driving the yawl boat then ferried Euretta back to shore, where she would likely rush off to pay the most urgent of her bills.

Under sail, *Marvel* followed a fluid itinerary, according to which way the wind was blowing. Meckling advertised the cruise as a "vagabond vacation," encouraging passengers to engage in a fantasy of serendipity. The first day was typically spent sailing south down the Bay past the old screwpile lighthouse at Thomas Point and perhaps over to Poplar Island on the Eastern Shore. After anchoring, if the crabs were swimming, the deckhands would delight the passengers on deck by netting a few dozen from the yawl boat. Pinky steamed the crabs and the group gathered for an al fresco Maryland crab feast on deck. The next day might take *Marvel* to St. Michaels, a quaint fishing village. Then on to Cambridge, a bustling port on the Choptank River. Overnighting in Cambridge gave the passengers an opportunity to go to a restaurant or take in a movie. There might be a stop at Oxford, a rich historical town, then a slow return to Annapolis. Other itineraries took *Marvel* back to the western shore, perhaps spending a night off Fairhaven, in Herring Bay or in the West River, near Shady Side and Galesville.

Levin J Marvel in West River

All summer, Kabernagel was keeping his eye on *Marvel*. Meckling suspected that he was being pursued at times by Pinkerton detectives. Patrols routinely followed *Marvel* to be sure it was sailing only under its own power and not with the assistance of the yawl boat that was always in tow, tied close behind the stern. Meckling did use the boat to aid in the forward progress while *Marvel* was sailing, but he was careful to keep it tucked up under the stern, running, unmanned, as if it was just bobbing along. He also tied a string to the ignition, just in case he needed to shut off the engine.

Evenings were especially pleasant aboard *Marvel*. The ship anchored most nights, and the passengers stayed on deck late into the night after one of Pinky's delicious meals, watching the Milky Way trail and sometimes singing. Sometimes, the fluid schedule made Meckling sail at night to get back to Annapolis in time for the disembarkation. Ghosting along on the quiet Bay held its own magic. The Old Bay Line night boat that ran between Baltimore and Norfolk often sought out the tall masts of *Marvel* and came toward the old ship to shine its spotlight on the sails and show its passengers the relic of the days of sail.

There was little for Kabernagel to find fault with aboard *Marvel*. The ship was apparently sound that summer. Its seams were freshly caulked, at least below the waterline. The weather was generally fair, and the food was excellent. But, in truth, *Marvel* was in rough shape. Meckling attempted to keep the paint fresh but there was no hiding the vessel's age and the fact that it had not been maintained. Perhaps that added to the allure of the ship for some of the passengers. It was, after all, an adventure cruise.

Unkempt to the Discerning Eye

But not to all. Amid the comings and goings of a Sunday afternoon, the Coast Guard was making an informal inspection of the Chesapeake Windjammer. Captain Phillip Overdon and Lt. Commander Blandon Harris, an inspector who traveled the country checking out Coast Guard-certified vessels, had heard the many conflicting stories about what Meckling was up to with the old ship. In their offices in Coast Guard headquarters in Washington, DC, Meckling's appeal of Kabernagel's "no sail," order was a topic of conversation.

"I'd like to take a look at this vessel," Overdon said. Harris, who had seen *Marvel* while on temporary assignment in the Chesapeake area, volunteered to drive Capt. Overdon out to Annapolis to take a look. Harris thought that a casual visit to the ship while docked in Annapolis would give them context for future discussion.

He and Overdon, who planned to just look around, wore civilian clothes on their visit to the ship while it was in port. Around 1pm, the two Coast Guard officers strolled along the pier where *Marvel* was docked, taking a close look at the hull. They walked from the stern to the bow and turned around and walked back to the stern and had a look at the yawl boat tied there. Harris, who had little experience with wooden boats, nevertheless saw loose planks and missing fasteners near the transom, causing it to bulge out. He pointed this out to Overdon, who was the Chief of Merchant Marine Safety Division of the U.S. Coast Guard.

On City Dock, the two men mingled with Sunday tourists, who were inevitably drawn to the towering masts of *Marvel*. As usual, the gangway was down and the two climbed aboard. Three or four other people were looking around on the deck, exploring the old ship. The two undercover inspectors strolled from stern to bow noticing the "unkempt" conditions and overall bad appearance the ship made. They took the steps in the bow and emerged in the hall of passenger cabins just as some of the passengers were getting settled in. Someone, probably not Meckling, approached the pair. They must have looked a bit out of place, an odd couple, roaming below decks. The friendly crewmember, or maybe an eager passenger, asked Harris if they would like a tour. Harris smiled and said, "No, thank you, we are just observing."

They went up the stern companionway stairs and exited the ship without identifying themselves.

They concluded they would not, under any circumstances, have taken a voyage on *Marvel*.

The Coast Guard officers' conclusion would be shared by another group who boarded *Marvel* that weekend.

Samuel Finkelstein, a Manhattan attorney, was one of the would-be adventurers who was lured by the promise of a "different sort of vacation." The brochure and marketing materials that Meckling purchased from Herman Knust along with the ship promised a taste of the romantic days of sail aboard a sturdy three-master that was compliant with all safety regulations. This last bit, while appealing directly to urbanites such as Finkelstein, was a bit of a stretch.

A Vacation "Adventure"
on
Chesapeake Bay

Brochure for Chesapeake Windjammer Cruises, c. 1947, showing a
much more commodious ship than *Marvel* of 1954-55

As Meckling knew, and the Coast Guard headquarters in Washington, D.C. affirmed, there were few applicable regulations to meet. So this claim might have qualified for, at least, misleading advertising.

The old brochure also promised comfortable amenities onboard, including "deck chairs for lounging" and "deck games such as shuffleboard." Photographs showed club-like leather seating in the lounge and sparkling white paint on the hull beneath crisp sails.

Finkelstein invited his wife's sister and her family to join them on a cruise. They would be a party of four adults and three children. After sending in their deposit, the group received a follow-up letter with the salutation "Ahoy Mateys!" It instructed passengers to feel free to arrive in Annapolis on Sunday and stay aboard *Marvel* before setting sail on Monday. The Finkelsteins took the captain up on the offer and headed to the ship after an early dinner in Washington, DC, about an hour's drive.

Finkelstein recalled being "stunned" by the "decrepit" appearance of *Marvel* at the pier in Annapolis. He had spent five years in the Army, so was not expecting first class accommodations. He and his family were expecting to rough it on the trip. But instead of a ship-shape vessel, Finkelstein saw an old hulk with piles of dirty line lying about. The captain was lounging on deck, although there were no deck chairs in evidence, with a woman he referred to as "Mother," who he correctly assumed was Euretta, and little Wayne.

As the Finkelsteins stowed their luggage below in cabins, they quickly realized some of the not-so-romantic parts of the age of sail. While tied up in a windless but bustling seaport, large sailing ships can be very hot. The heat on that first weekend of September was oppressive in Annapolis. The single porthole in each cabin needed to be open to catch any breath of air, but bugs came aboard through them. The harbor, filled with waterman's workboats just in from catching crabs and fish, contributed to a fetid feast for flies and seagulls.

The Finkelstein party decided to abandon ship after a long, sleepless, not to mention, buggy, night spent on deck. The group took their leave from *Marvel* about two hours before the scheduled sailing time of 10am on Monday. They gathered their bags and left Annapolis without seeing Captain Meckling, who was apparently on a last-minute errand.

These were the exceptions to the rule that summer. Generally, people were charmed by the adventure, won over by Meckling and convinced by the sheer size of the ship of its stability.

Preparing for Season Two

After seven cruises in the summer of 1954, John and Euretta Meckling had devised a successful formula. Meckling's personality and confidence convinced even skeptical passengers that a vagabond adventure on *Marvel* was exactly the antidote for their stress-filled city lives. Young single women were particularly enamored of the sandy-haired captain, who let them have a hand at steering the big ship. There were customers who booked a second and even a third back-to-back voyage. The season ended with plenty of bookings for the summer of 1955 in place.

Even with high occupancy rates, Meckling found it difficult to make ends meet. The expenses of running a vessel of the size and age of *Marvel* were more than tickets brought in. Beyond that, Meckling did not have the sharp pencil he needed to maximize receipts. So repairs in the 1954–1955 off-season were limited to what he could afford.

Meckling did as much as he could on the ship by himself. He had several projects underway at any given time. The old ship needed a serious overhaul but that meant drydocking or hauling it and the money did not exist for that level of repair and maintenance. Instead, Meckling worked on keeping up appearances. He painted, replaced rotted planks and "rejuvenated," as he put it, the passenger staterooms. But even that effort fell a bit short. His paint scheme on the boat included an aluminum silver paint that was out of sync with the white and buff of other vessels of that day. Meckling probably found the paint for a good price and reasoned that the modern paint would indicate recent painting.

In addition to working on the boat that winter, Meckling made an alliance with Victor Frankel, a Baltimore developer who was building a community of single-family homes in Annapolis away from the cramped downtown district. Ever talented, Meckling convinced Frankel to hire him as a building superintendent and surveyor for the project, a deal that gave him one of the homes. Thus, during the sailing season, Euretta and Wayne—who lived on the boat that first winter—would have a home.

The Mecklings were optimistic as *Marvel's* 1955 season began.

Meckling Rounds Out The Crew

In the spring of 1955, high school kids were cruising around town in their parents' cars, listening to rock and roll. Bill Verge and Steve MacDougall were right there with them. The teenagers had just completed their junior year at a prep school near Annapolis, Maryland. Verge, the son of a retired Navy admiral, and MacDougall, the stepson of a wealthy jetsetter, had become fast friends at the Severn School, which at the time, served as the prep

Severn School, junior class, 1955

school for the U.S. Naval Academy. They were not exactly renegades; they were comfortable in their khakis and blazers. But the starched white uniforms of the Academy were a different story. If their destiny was to become midshipmen, they would be joining the ranks just weeks after graduating high school. The summer of '55 promised freedom, maybe for the last time.

Bill and Steve even had the unheard-of luxury of their own apartment, albeit under the eye of Steve's grandmother. The Verge family was relocating to Florida that summer, and Steve's mother and stepfather were always on their own travel schedule. The two boys moved in with Steve's maternal grandmother. Lucile "Lou" Hamel Burtis was not a typical 1950s' grandmother. A retired dancer who had been part of the famed Ziegfeld Follies musical revue in New York City, she was a cosmopolitan woman who enjoyed having the young people's company. The feeling was mutual. The boys dubbed the spacious downtown Annapolis apartment "Club 73" for its address: 73 Maryland Avenue. The arrangement worked out well for both families. Bill's father left the old family car, so they had wheels. As school wound down, the two went off to look for jobs to finance their summer of independence.

In their quest for work and excitement, Bill and Steve visited Annapolis City Dock. At the end of the bulkhead, *Levin J Marvel*'s three masts towered over the fleet of crabbing boats and skipjacks tied three abreast in a dingy juxtaposition to the gleaming boats at the Annapolis Yacht Club and shipshape training vessels of the U.S. Naval Academy.

The teens had grown up in the yachting circles of Annapolis; they had raced and crewed with their parents on sailing vacations. But this boat was different. At 128 feet with a bowsprit reaching out another 50 feet, and 90-foot Georgia pine masts webbed with rigging and lines, this was a pirate ship, and that was just what these two were looking for.

On that spring day at the end of May, *Levin J Marvel* was preparing to venture out for her first full season of cruises. John Meckling, the sandy-haired captain, himself a bit of a renegade, was alone on deck sanding a hatch cover. Bill called up to him.

"Captain, you have any work for us?"

"You boys come on up here," he said, affecting gruffness, not looking up from his work.

They climbed the gangway and made their way across a deck covered in piles of lines, buckets and boards.

"You boys don't even know how to ask for a job," Meckling growled good-naturedly. Looking over at the chastened boys, he turned playful.

"Can you sail? Of course, you can...look at you. Come down tomorrow and we will take you out on a shakedown. Pack your sea bag." With that, both boys' lives were put on a new course. They wouldn't be going to the Naval Academy; in fact, they would not even be returning to finish high school in the fall.

It was foggy and misting a light rain when Bill and Steve walked to the docks the following evening. The town was eerily quiet. Never had their colonial town's ghosts—Lafayette and Washington had walked these streets together almost two centuries before—been so present to them.

Once onboard the old ship, they were quickly approved for service. There was no need for further interviews:

both boys were sailors, good-looking and had prep school manners. It was classic John Meckling, to sail with an unknown green crew on the first trip of the season, as always, confident that he made the right call.

The first passengers boarded the following day.

Levin J Marvel spies a freighter.

The new crew learned the ropes, both literally and figuratively, on the job. The ship sailed well, albeit slowly, which was lucky, because it gave them time to adjust when they made mistakes. They learned how the donkey engine could assist in raising the great sails. Or, on one occasion, hoist Bill halfway up the mast when a line slipped off. They learned to use the yawl boat to assist in docking and undocking the great ship. A third deckhand often sailed with them. A local waterman, known only as Mooney, taught them tricks from his years on the rough workboats.

Bill felt an immediate affinity to John Meckling. Meckling was an adventurous entrepreneur, a self-taught jack-of-all-trades, a role model for the young adventure-seekers. He made light of difficult situations and put faith in his own ability to solve them. When he stepped on *Marvel*, Bill stepped out from the long shadow of his decorated war-hero father. The young man found the rough living on the ship suited him. He did not mind the hard work of being the ship's "maintenance man," as he thought of himself. Standing watches and sleeping in the sail locker or on deck was just fine by Bill.

Steve's relationship with Meckling was more nuanced. He had sailed offshore with his stepfather, and was, at times, uneasy with Meckling's devil-may-care seamanship. But perhaps at the root of Steve's suspicion was a quality of rakishness Meckling shared with his stepfather. Steve MacDougall was called Steve Morton that summer, temporarily using the name of his mother Josephine's husband. As he approached 18 and joined the Coast Guard, he reverted to his legal name, MacDougall.

Each weekend, the pair returned to the apartment at Maryland Avenue and spent Saturday and Sunday cruising around town, feeling much older than their high school friends. They made $25 each week on *Marvel* and spent it mostly on beer each weekend. Steve had taken to wearing a coonskin cap over his blonde hair and onboard had become known as "Davy," for Davy Crockett, a popular folk hero in 1955. As they found new identities, the boys both decided that they were not returning to complete high school at the Severn School. The two were no longer schoolboys but mariners, admired by the young passengers and treated as valuable crewmen by their captain.

Elry Pinkney, the ship's cook, took the boys under his wing and became the jocular uncle just as Meckling had become the older brother Bill had never had. A savvy African American in a Jim Crow town, Pinky knew how to play by the rules and play the rules. Pinky taught the deck hands how to be both present and invisible around the passengers. He took them to market to provision each cruise, making sure to buy their favorite treats. He taught them card tricks and kitchen hacks. He knew just when to whip out a delicious batch of cookies when the passengers were getting restive on a long sail.

As for passengers, Meckling had a rule that he may or may not have abided by. He asked the boys on deck that day in their impromptu interview what they would do if a beautiful girl asked them to come to her cabin. They looked at one another, not sure how to answer. Meckling winked and said, "You better stay away! No fraternizing with the guests!"

Bill and Steve were too busy most of the time to worry about beautiful women. There were a multitude of chores every day aboard *Marvel*. The sails alone took almost an hour to set. There were days when the wind was light, as it often is during a Chesapeake summer. Steve or Bill jumped into the yawl boat and, being careful to stay low, in case Coast Guard was watching, tucked up under the stern and pushed the old behemoth toward the next stop.

It became clear to Bill that Meckling did not have the funds to keep up with the day-to-day maintenance of the old ship, let alone the major work that would be required in the off-season. He imagined he and Steve could take over where Meckling left off and return *Marvel* to service more in keeping with the clientele's expectations. Bill began to take stock of the ship with a more critical eye. He made calculations, balancing expenses with potential revenue. Starting a business with Steve seemed like a practical move. If not *Marvel*, maybe another ship.

He and Steve also visited *Jennie D Bell* and her septuagenarian owners, one weekend, hoping they might be ready to sell. Captain and Mrs. Heath met with Steve and Bill in the cozy cabin of their schooner home. They wished the young fellows well but were not ready to retire "yet awhile." The young visionaries returned their focus to *Levin J Marvel* as an enterprise devoted to escape, both for the city-dwelling dude cruisers and for themselves.

Financing would not be the problem that it was for Meckling. Bill spoke to his uncle, a prominent attorney in Baltimore and an avid sailor. He convinced his uncle of the viability of the business if there was actual money behind it. After all, Meckling's shoestring operation was actually quite successful. Cabins were filled or nearly filled on each cruise. Even so, Meckling was facing a financial reality check as the season rolled on. While he was a remarkable problem solver when it came to mechanical issues on the ship, the bookkeeping eluded him. He often gave discounted fares to those passengers he liked, thinking it might bring more business.

Knowing he had a family to support, Meckling was ready to turn over the helm of his fanciful dream boat. The boys' practical plan was not to sail the ship themselves but to hire someone knowledgeable and reliable, like Bob Shores, the relief captain who once worked for Herman Knust. Bill had visited the Booz Brother's shipyard to get their assessment of the vessel when it was hauled the prior year. He put on his swim trunks and made multiple underwater inspections of his own. Finally, he prepared a proposal to present in August to his uncle and a group of potential investors in the third iteration of Chesapeake Windjammer Vacations. That meeting would keep him from *Marvel's* last voyage.

Omen from on High

The height of the summer was marked by a large group of high school students who came from Dayton, Ohio. The Traveling University Program booked the entire ship for a weeklong educational tour. Some 50 students and adults crowded aboard *Marvel*. During the visits to port, the students saw the sights and completed assignments that took them to visit local businesses and government buildings. They reassembled onboard in the late afternoons, and each group shared their findings. The teens spent their evenings listening to the radio and sneaking around their chaperones into one another's cabins. Come morning, they were late risers.

The Traveling University, a church youth group from Dayton, Ohio on *Levin J Marvel,* July, 1955

Bleary eyed or not, the young students should enjoy at least one sunrise on the Bay, their pastor decided. Bill and Steve roused the passengers as ordered, just before daybreak, with the call all hands on deck. As the sleepy ship's company assembled to view the sunrise on the Chesapeake, the pastor pointed out what he called a "message" from above. Three seagulls sailed across the rising sun, flying from left to right on the horizon. "Faith, hope and charity," the landlubber intoned earnestly. Bill and John Meckling exchanged glances. They knew that in the tradition of seafaring men, three seagulls in flight across the rising sun deliver a very different message, an omen of bad luck.

Part II:

THE STORM

Here's A...
"Different Vacation"
Cruising The Historic
Chesapeake Bay

A NEW VACATION "ADVENTURE"
FOR YOU!

Aboard Our
128 Foot Three-Masted Schooners
"LEVIN J. MARVEL" and "EDWIN & MAUD"

CHAPTER SEVEN

All Aboard

Excursions on *Marvel* were advertised as "A Different Sort of Vacation" and "Carefree Days on the Bay." The slogans had been created by a professional. Lester Trott—a well-known Annapolis ad man who directed the State of Maryland's tourism pitch in the 1960s—knew how to attract customers. For Herman Knust, he created a suite of ads for print media in metropolitan areas within driving distance to Annapolis. The ads ran heavily and successfully in the New York market. With Meckling as with Knust, passengers were often New Yorkers who had a sense of adventure and enough money and time to take a week off.

The passengers who boarded *Marvel* Sunday, August 7, 1955, were especially dynamic. There were 23 in all, including several couples, a family of four, a father and son and young single professionals. By chance, there were two luminaries from the social sciences onboard. Bertram Roberts, a psychiatrist and researcher from Yale University, was working on the seminal research into the effects of social and birth order on mental health. Louis Sobel was a world-renowned advocate for children.

Minna and Louis Sobel

Louis Sobel and his wife Minna made up one of the couples. To the Sobels, recreational boating was a novelty. They lived on Central Park in Manhattan and were more accustomed to society gatherings than adventure travel. Louis had been secretary of the American Joint Distribution Agency, directing millions of dollars in relief to the Jewish victims of World War II. The Washington, D.C. Agency provided free loans to German Jews to aid them in surviving in Germany and Poland under the Nazi regime. It also assisted in emigration of refugees and supported the families' resettlement.

Minna and Louis Sobel

In 1947, Sobel returned his family to New York, where he took the helm of the largest child-care organization in the U.S., the Jewish Child Care Association. This group pioneered in child welfare, founding the first psychiatric clinic within an orphanage in recognition of the mental trauma of young people. Sobel's work with refugees and the families in need would have been of special interest to Bert Roberts, who was studying these same populations.

Bertram and Frances Roberts

Bert Roberts and his wife Frances traveled to *Marvel* from New Haven, Connecticut, where he taught and conducted research at Yale University. They had led charmed lives. A native of Toronto, Roberts emigrated to the U.S. after taking his undergraduate degree at Columbia University. He went on to become a doctor, then trained as a psychiatrist and earned a master's degree in public health. The effects of social milieu on mental health were his special interest. Keen to learn about Freudian analysis, he regularly caught the train to Manhattan to pursue his own analysis.

Bertram and Frances Roberts

Frances and Bert were well-matched intellectually. A Vassar grad who pursued a master's degree at Yale in education, she was also beautiful. She and Bert had honeymooned in Bermuda, the first and last vacation of their marriage. This summer would break the pattern. They planned to join Roberts' Yale psychiatry colleagues for a week at the beach on Cape Cod. A nanny was lined up to stay with their two daughters, a toddler and a six-month-old, Maggie and Priscilla. But a polio outbreak on the Cape changed their plans. With the time set aside for a trip, the Roberts cast about for another getaway. They settled on the *Levin J Marvel* cruise after seeing an ad in the New York Times. The promise of a "Different Sort of Vacation" appealed to the Roberts' intellectual sensibilities.

Bert and Frances took the train south with their bags packed for a week on the water. But when they reached the Annapolis harbor and saw the peeling *Marvel*, they wondered whether their decision had been wise. To have time to reflect and discuss, they volunteered to get provisions in town. After a walk around downtown Annapolis, Bert convinced Frances to reboard *Marvel*, saying, "If Louis Sobel is onboard, it has to be safe, and think of the conversations we will have."

Dr. Andrew Chesson and Girlie Compton Chesson

Andrew Chesson and his wife traveled from Raleigh, North Carolina. The trip was a celebration of Girlie's recovery. She had been confined to bed for most of the spring of 1955 with an illness.

The Chessons, parents of Andy, 6, and Peggy, 4, were well known and respected in church and social circles in the small city. Andrew Chesson was held in special renown. As a young surgeon with an interest in the brain and neurology, he had founded the Cerebral Palsy Clinic in Raleigh. Rising to positions of staff leadership in the hospital where he practiced, he had gone on to the unheard-of position of chief of staff of two Raleigh hospitals by the time he and his wife took a well-deserved vacation to the Chesapeake. He would have had a good conversational partner in Bert Roberts. Girlie would have found a companion in Frances Roberts, as they were both young mothers.

Nancy Sawyer Sevier Madden

Nancy Sawyer Sevier Madden made the trip on her own. A 33-year-old Kansas native, she was the unusual woman graduate of the prestigious journalism program at the University of Iowa, the class of 1942. Women journalists of this era were limited to reporting on fashion and lifestyle; Madden veered to a career in advertising in Washington, D.C. Like her education, her sensibilities were more modern than her 1950s' peers. Active and athletic, she took pride in eschewing car ownership. Instead, she maintained her fitness by walking everywhere in Washington.

Madden was also a history buff. Her family on both sides descended from a Revolutionary War hero and governor of Tennessee, John Sevier. The" Father of Tennessee" had a story worth telling: his bitter and contentious relationship with president-to-be Andrew Jackson.

MISS NANCY MADDEN
Survives Shipwreck

Sevier and Jackson were both titanic figures in the frontier lands. Sevier served two separate terms as governor, elected the second time even amid a scandal promulgated by Jackson. Their malice grew dangerous in 1803. Their egos matched with their wits were well suited to uncensored and colorful insults. On the steps of the courthouse in Knoxville, where Jackson was then a judge, Sevier offered an insult that Jackson could not leave unanswered within the strict code of honor of the ruling class. The governor goaded the judge about his lack of military service. Jackson shot back about his "Many services to the state and the nation." Sevier then took a mocking tone and said, in front of a growing crowd of onlookers, "Services? I know of no services besides taking a trip to Natchez with another man's wife." This took the confrontation to a new level.

The following day Jackson added new insults. "The ungentlemanly expressions and gasconading conduct to me yesterday was in true character of yourself." Sevier responded to the letter, once again mocking Jackson by throwing the barbs back at him and correcting his grammar. The challenge was too great to ignore. As dueling was illegal in Tennessee, they agreed to meet in the boundary lands near the Indian Territory.

What happened in the confrontation on October 16, 1803 is unclear because only partisan reports remain. What is clear is that neither fired, although it appears Jackson, brandishing a cane, charged Sevier on horseback. The affair ended in a handshake and continued political animus for years to come.

Researching and writing the Sevier family history, running to 558 pages, would take Madden and her coauthor a quarter of a century. It is known in the world of genealogy as a masterpiece of research accomplished before internet resources made genealogy easier.

Madden came aboard *Levin J Marvel* well-prepared for a week of adventure. This type of vacation was just the style of this free-thinking, engaging conversationalist. She had packed her red swimsuit, a yellow slicker and floppy sou'wester rainhat that might later save her life.

Harry "Zimmie" Nathanson

Harry "Zimmie" Nathanson was a 38-year-old physical education teacher from Lawrence, New York, outside of

New York City. He had sailed twice before on Knust's *Levin J Marvel* some six years earlier. He convinced his best friend, Harry Kirsener, to join him for a third cruise on the Chesapeake. The *Marvel* he saw when he arrived in Annapolis was a disappointment to him. It bore little resemblance to the ship he had enthused about. That boat, he later recalled, "looked slick and white in the water, despite her 60-odd years. Now the sides of her hull were black and dirty, and she didn't have that crisp look anymore."

Deborah Killip

Debbie was the youngest of the single passengers at 26. She was a junior copy writer at the Charles Rumrill agency in Rochester, New York. It was a good job, with plenty of opportunities for advancement. The agency was on top in a town dominated by the Eastman Kodak Company. That icon of photography was a magnet for creative professionals. Rumrill capitalized on the talent, making a perfect home for Debbie Killip, who was energetic and adventurous herself.

Debbie lived at home with her parents in the leafy suburb of Irondequoit. Her lakefront town provided her with ample opportunities for water-borne amusement. She was an able boater and swimmer. With her bobbing blonde hair and quick laugh, she quickly made friends on the ship. She also carried the charm of being the beloved only child, seeking companionship but not craving attention.

John Ferguson Senior and Junior

Another eager cruiser was John Ferguson, a 16-year old from Bloomfield, New Jersey, traveling with his father, John Sr. The younger John kept a diary of the vacation he had planned himself. They started off a day early so they could do some sightseeing in Washington, D.C. before boarding *Marvel* in Annapolis on August 7.

John Ferguson, Jr.
Dad Died in Tragedy

John Ferguson, Jr.

"Took cab to Penn Station (New York). Got 8:45 train. Passed through Trenton, Philadelphia, Wilmington, Baltimore. Arrived Union Station Washington at around 12:20. Got cab to Mayflower Hotel, very nice, had lunch in the lobby. Took Grayline sightseeing tour, picked us up in a '55 Cadillac."

On the tour, they saw the U.S. Marine Corps Memorial depicting the iconic photograph of six marines raising the American flag at Iwo Jima. President Dwight D. Eisenhower had dedicated the memorial just months ago. After the long day, they dined in the hotel.

The morning of August 7, John and his father grabbed orange juice and headed to Mass at the Cathedral of St. Matthew the Apostle, an 1893 church just a three-minute walk from the Mayflower. Then they headed to Annapolis. Young John's excitement was stoked.

John's idea for a boating excursion began with the Sunday *New York Times* travel section. Ads for the Maine windjammers intrigued the high school junior. He asked his father, an engineer who commuted to Manhattan from their home in northern New Jersey, if they might make a trip the next summer. John was mature for his age and, having grown up as the only at-home child of older parents, was used to being on his own with his imagination. Old sailing ships and boats in general fascinated him. He loved the family's vacations to the Jersey Shore, where they kept a small fishing boat. Happy to see his son's initiative, John senior agreed to the trip, putting down a deposit for the trip to Maine.

But then, John saw the ads for *Levin J Marvel* and had a change of heart. Here was a chance to visit several colonial towns that interested him as well as go on a sailing adventure. With his father's approval, the plan was changed.

When the Fergusons arrived at *Marvel*, however, John was disappointed. An avid reader of all things maritime,

John knew that the dull aluminum paint that covered the hull of the old ship was historical perjury.

His disappointment with the ship's appearance was forgotten when he climbed aboard and began to meet the rest of what he called in his diary, "the ship's company." He felt special kinship with deckhand Steve MacDougall, just a little older than himself, who was ably squaring away the ship to sail.

With an afternoon to spend on their own before sailing, the Fergusons wandered the narrow colonial streets of Annapolis in search of the Elks Club. Mr. Ferguson, a member of the club at home in New Jersey, enjoyed seeking out lodges in communities he visited. The lodge in Annapolis would have been a special treat. Like so much of the town, it oozed with history. The lodge was in the historic 1798 Franklin House. Annapolis was laid out with two adjacent circles, Church Circle, anchored by St. Anne's Episcopal Church, and State Circle, anchored by the State House, with the largest wooden dome in America. Around the circle, the business of government sprang up. The law office of James Franklin on Chancellery Lane was one of them. The Elks Lodge acquired the building in 1900. Over the years, the lodge had expanded to include adjoining buildings that faced Main Street. Young John loved the colonial architecture and Greek revival elements of the old building.

Almost immediately on returning to the ship in the late afternoon, John joined a "safari" to Mills Fine Wines and Spirits with a group of passengers. Evidently, the party was already starting. This well-heeled crew did not go in for

Mr. Donner's exquisite collection of wine that day; they were setting off on pirate adventure. John wrote, "Each man carried a case of beer and the blonde carried a bottle of rum, I came along with Pepsi."

When they got back to *Marvel*, some of the women were jumping rope on deck, which John found hilarious. They were probably just amusing the youngest passenger, Hillary Nevin, an 9-year-old who was aboard with her parents, and her 13-year-old brother, Hillard.

Filling Out the Ship's Company

Another medical doctor on the ship, Walter Goldstone, practiced at the Prospect Heights Hospital in Brooklyn, within walking distance from his home. He lived with his sister, Florence, in a rather grand limestone building near Prospect Park. Florence and Walter Goldstone were 40 and 37 when they decided to take a cruise on *Marvel*.

Bill Balle took trips on both the ram schooners. He sailed on *Edwin and Maud* under Herman Knust's command and made the acquaintance of Captain John Meckling during the 1954 season. He was a jovial New Yorker who relished time in the open air on the deck of the ship as it sailed. An enthusiastic sailor, he got a $10 discount as a repeat customer. Two single New Yorkers, Meryle Hutchinson and Charles Greenwald, went to Annapolis separately and quickly became companionable shipmates. We don't know much about Rhoda Fedder, the "blonde" who was toting the rum, except that she was 48 when she boarded *Marvel* alone. She lived in Greenwich

Village in Manhattan overlooking Washington Square Park. We can imagine her as a professor at NYU, or a beat-generation poet.

The 23 passengers who came together that Sunday evening were fairly typical of those attracted to a "dude cruise" aboard *Marvel*. They were moderately affluent, open-minded adventurous spirits, maybe a bit romantic.

Underway

Marvel and its passengers left Annapolis in a drizzle on Monday, August 8. Bill Verge was not aboard because he was meeting with potential investors in Baltimore that week. He came to the dock only to assist with getting underway, then left with plans to rejoin the crew later in the week. This left just Meckling and Steve to run the ship. The ship set out for an easy day sail to its first anchorage, Poplar Island.

By 1955, the island was uninhabited. The few hundred residents had left for the mainland in the early 1920s. Erosion, probably caused by the island's sawmill business, ate away homes and farmland. Bootleggers took over the island until a raid in 1929. The island also had a hunting lodge that later hosted Presidents Roosevelt and Truman. That, too, was in ruins by 1955, when and the island made a good wind break for *Marvel's* first anchorage.

John Ferguson had a wonderful first day under sail, imagining he was headed for the South Pacific. In the evening, the weather had cleared and the younger of the ship's company spent the evening on deck, getting to know one another.

On Tuesday, *Marvel* made a short sail to the Eastern Shore towns of Oxford and Bellevue. John Ferguson visited an antique store in Bellevue and found a ship in a bottle to take home as a souvenir. In the evening, most of the passengers walked from the municipal dock in Oxford to the historic Robert Morris Inn, had a drink in the colonial tavern and watched "Dragnet" on television.

By then, Hurricane Connie was a distant presence. A storm with an uncertain track, it was anticipated to make landfall somewhere along the East Coast later in that second week of August. But with the ship always within sight of shore, the hurricane was merely news on the radio. There was no great concern as of yet. Steve McDougall, though, was apprehensive about the voyage's timing from the start. His concern grew as the week wore on. It was difficult raising and striking sails without Bill's help. If things got too snotty, he would be in trouble. On Tuesday night as they bedded down in Oxford, Meckling, who was glued to the marine weather forecasts, decided to move the boat to Cambridge. This was a sensible choice, the commercial dock was heavier, the city was farther up the river and more protected, and it would offer more amusements to the city folk.

Passengers and crew woke up in Cambridge Thursday to a beautiful Chesapeake morning.

A. Aubrey Bodine

Thur ~~Sat~~
~~Fri~~

August ~~12~~ 11, 1955

What a day! Wow!
Breakfast. Went aboard
Potomac. Sailed from
Cambridge for swimming.
Dropped hook in 20 ft
of water. Everybody went
in water. Paddled float
around LJ. M got in to
ruble off stern of yawl
boat. Made it alright.
Lunch. Set sail. Had
great undersail again
Then the real fun start-
ed. Bill wanted to
go to Oxford in th
yawl boat to l
in liquid supplies
party tomorrow n
I went along. Bill
self, Hilliard h

CHAPTER EIGHT

"Wow! What a Day!" —A Great Trip Ends in Disaster as *Marvel* Founders

Thursday morning began the day that John Ferguson would reflect upon that night as the "most exciting day so far." The morning was clear and sunny, the best weather day on the voyage. The dock in Cambridge was close enough to town that people went for a walk in the early morning sunshine. It appeared, from radio reports, that Hurricane Connie was headed away from the coast. The day was off to a promising start.

As steward Charles Savoy came back from a trip to get fresh stores for dinner, he saw that the Cambridge Yacht Club had taken down the red-and-black hurricane warning flags. Meckling walked over and chatted with the yacht club manager, who was receiving the bulletins from the weather bureau. The noon weather forecast on the radio caused cheers to erupt onboard. The hurricane seemed to have indeed veered away from land, and hurricane warnings were taken down for Chesapeake Bay. Storm warnings remained, as northeast winds were predicted to gust to up to 40mph.

Decisions made in a moment, when viewed through the lens of retrospect, are sometimes hard to justify. Such was John Meckling's decision to sail from Cambridge that day. Worse in retrospect was his failure to run to Annapolis as quickly as possible during the window of fine weather that morning through midday. Instead, to please his guests, they lingered for a swim on the northern side of the Choptank River. Meckling tarried, eager to let his passengers enjoy one last day. He would take off in the afternoon for the sail back to the western shore and make Annapolis by morning.

Bill Verge, the missing deckhand, called the yacht club on Thursday to locate *Marvel* so he could rejoin the crew. He was alarmed to learn that the ship had sailed, for he was very worried about the weather. Even though the storm was apparently moving away, surely there would be a blow, and Steve was going to have his hands full. He debated driving to the Eastern Shore to catch them, but how? The meetings set up with potential investors had gone well, and Bill was confident that he and Steve would make good partners in the venture. But now, he was facing the worrisome prospect of the ship making it home safely.

After a picnic lunch and a swim, *Marvel* started on its last sail. Meckling was anticipating a smooth trip down the Choptank to the Bay, then an overnight into Annapolis. There was one pressing matter for the passengers, however. Liquor was running low. Bill Balle, the ringleader of the party crowd, requested a yawl boat excursion into Oxford to stock up.

"That is when the real fun started," wrote John Ferguson that night in his diary. Steve fired up the yawl boat to make a quick trip into Oxford, the closest port

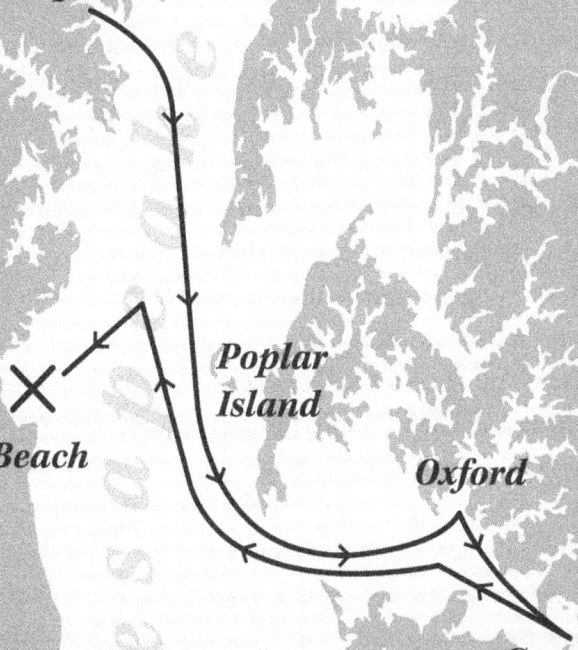

Chesapeake Bay

Annapolis

North Beach

Poplar
Island

Oxford

Cambridge

to slow-moving *Marvel*. They would gather supplies and intercept the ship. John Ferguson, 13-year-old Hillard Nevin and his father, Hillard Sr., joined in the adventure.

According to John's diary, the yawl boat was having some transmission problems during the booze run. Steve could not shift the motor into reverse to slow down the approach to the dock. They wound up slamming into it. Back at the ship, Meckling worked on the finicky transmission on the engine that had been pulled from an old Lincoln automobile.

Progress was slow as the ship moved down the Choptank. The wind never picked up as predicted. Old *Marvel* barely moved in the light breeze; it was midnight before they saw Sharps Island Lighthouse. This lighthouse marks the Choptank River, and is about 30 miles from Annapolis harbor, as the crow flies.

Several passengers—including Harry Nathanson, Harry Kirsener, Perry Schwartz, Debbie Killip and Nancy Madden—stayed on deck as late as 2am looking at the stars. They followed *Marvel's* slow progress on a chart as they passed each marker in the Choptank River. In his cabin, John Ferguson related the day's adventure under the opening line, "What a day!"

The captain turned off the radio at 11pm so the guests below could sleep. It was unfortunate timing because he missed more current weather forecasts, which were not good. Connie had turned inland and was now tracking a course up the Chesapeake. From drifting along at one knot, the ship sped up in the middle of the night. Under the freshening breeze, Steve scrambled to adjust the sail set on three masts and secure gear on deck. The yawl boat was, as usual, towing along.

The wind steadily strengthened in the pre-dawn hours as the outermost bands of wind from Connie reached *Marvel*. These were gusty winds, challenging the old canvas. They needed to shorten the sails. As Steve struggled to do this by himself, Meckling came to the dining room as the passengers were having breakfast and asked volunteers to assist in getting the sails furled. Harry Nathanson, the fit gym teacher, came on deck to help—unaware he was just beginning a long day of working as a deckhand. Others came to help Nathanson and Steve as they wrestled with the main sail. Close to one thousand pounds of canvas flapped wildly on the deck, lines snapping against the wind

Finally, the sails were under control. The ship was now sailing under just one sail, on the third mast aft, known as the "spanker," and a small staysail. Still, Meckling struggled to keep a course across the Bay.

The heavy wind blowing from the northeast made northerly progress toward Annapolis impossible. Instead, Meckling backtracked toward Poplar Island, reasoning that they could ride out the wind in the protection of the channel behind the island.

Even that slight northerly turn was not possible under just the one sail. Heavy old *Marvel* was barreling into the main channel of the Chesapeake. This course was almost straight across from the West River, which would provide plenty of hurricane holes to ride out any storm and was closer to the final destination. That became the new destination.

Meckling told the Associated Press, in an interview two days later, what happened next:

> *With each gust, the ship would heel way over. We suddenly were struck by a 40–50 mile an hour gust that removed all canvas from the vessel. We had no sail aloft, we turned broadside to the seas...When we saw it would be impossible to reach West River, we headed for Herring Bay. It was about 10am. By this time the visibility was about 300 yards. The wind and rain had whipped up a mist off the sea and it was like looking at a white wall.*

Holed Up In Herring Bay

Herring Bay is about five miles south of the West River. Barely an indent on the shoreline, it is certainly not a harbor. This shallow bay, surrounded by a long sandbar and rock jetties, became Meckling's only choice to anchor and ride out the storm. *Marvel* had run out of options, and the winds kept increasing.

Meckling sent Steve to climb into the yawl boat to help push *Marvel* to get some steering control. The engine would not start, for all Steve's cranking. With the boat half-filled with water in the wild crossing, the engine had been submerged. The yawl boat was of no use now.

Although Meckling told the AP reporter that he had no sails, he probably meant that he had taken down the large sails and was steering by the staysail. He knew Herring Bay well. He was able to avoid the sandbar and find a spot to anchor. They dropped anchor at around 11:30am and breathed a sigh of relief. Pinky served up cold sandwiches to the group gathered in the lounge. These people had been strangers in the beginning of the cruise, but now were a team, concerned for one another's safety. The mood remained light even as conditions worsened. Young John worried that if they didn't hurry up and get safely back to Annapolis, his father might rescind his permission to stay on *Marvel* for another week.

Survivors later wondered at the lack of panic among the passengers. Instead, they pitched in to help wherever they could. People went below and began grabbing lifejackets.

Connie continued to beat on the old 128-foot hull. Large waves were breaking across the deck, and the green water was pouring down below as well as coming in through the hull. *Marvel's* bilge pumps were overwhelmed. Men took turns working handpumps. A portable gasoline pump helped, but someone needed to constantly keep it from clogging.

Perry Schwartz—electronics engineer from Clifton, New Jersey, and a ham radio enthusiast—took to the radio. The radio had worked all summer, but when Meckling called for help after entering Herring Bay, he was unable to transmit a Mayday. As Schwartz attempted to find the problem with the radio, he continued transmitting a Mayday call. He got no response to his transmissions.

Onshore, people were also surprised by Connie's forceful entrance onto the scene. At the small marina

Norman Marshall ran in Deale, just to the north of Herring Bay on Rockhold Creek, pleasure boats and workboats tied up on the docks were rocking violently, straining at their lines. On most any other summer day, the marina was a quiet place. During the week, workboats returned from checking their crab pots in the mid to late morning. The sailboats kept by out-of-towners were still, and only sound would be Marshall working on an engine or the ospreys whistling overhead, marking their territory.

On August 12, however, the wind was whipping up whitecaps in Rockhold Creek, water piling in from the Bay. Wind was howling through the rigging on the boats, clattering and crashing, making it difficult to hear. Marshall's son Thomas, 18 that summer, was scrambling to help slack lines that were put under tremendous strain by the rapidly increasing seas and high tide. The docks were covered with nearly a foot of water; it was dangerous work. Marshall had to scream to be heard as he sent Thomas to the shed on shore to get more lines. Thomas ran up to the shed, barefoot, using his feet to feel where the pier ended, and the land began. He was gathering up lines in the shed, and the wind was howling. Scared, he took a few minutes to collect himself before going back out into the soaking rain and howling wind.

In those minutes, the Zenith Transoceanic radio, mounted above the worktable and tuned to the Coast Guard 2182 megahertz, crackled. It was always on in the marina. Today, Thomas heard a clear voice calling through the static, "Mayday, Mayday, Mayday, this is the *Levin J Marvel...*" Stopping to listen, he heard the same voice repeat the call. He had never heard a call like that before; he had no idea what it meant. Some official transmission related to the severe weather, he assumed.

Thomas had already left his father alone too long on the docks. He closed the door and walked out, mentioning nothing to his father until later on, in the house, when the wind was still blowing but the boats were safe, for the moment. Assuming the kid had misheard the call for help, Marshall also dismissed it.

Final Minutes

On *Marvel*, the scene was getting more and more chaotic.

Survivors had varying recollections of Connie's final blow to *Marvel*. The anchor began to drag the ship closer toward the shallows. Somehow, as water built up in the bow, pulling it down, Meckling and Steve managed to reset it. Steve deployed a second anchor from the bow on the opposite side. They hoped the two anchors might keep the ship from being pushed broadside to the seas because it would only be able to turn so far and then be stopped by the opposing anchor. This may have been a deadly decision; the old vessel's structural timbers were so weak that the opposing forces might have pulled them apart.

The men aboard continued fighting the inflow of the Bay, hand pumping or working the one gasoline pump still functioning. But the seas were quickly overtaking their efforts. John Ferguson and his father went below, where they found water pouring in through the portholes.

They attempted to secure the open ports, but some had missing wingnuts, and some were stuck. To staunch what water he could, John stuffed blankets into the portholes. With water rising quickly in the cabins, John's father said, "This is getting serious."

Meckling now realized saving *Marvel* was out of the question and focused on saving the passengers. It was time to abandon ship.

Several years earlier, while sailing with two friends on an old wooden skiff, they were caught out in a violent summer squall. The sailboat began to take on water. As it sank, the three friends put on their lifebelts and threaded a line between them, tying themselves together. They went into the water together and waited out the squall. When they could see where they were, and they made their way to shore in unison.

Meckling recalled that day as he realized that *Marvel* might not survive this storm. He estimated it was about a mile and a half to shore. In the wind and waves, it would be difficult to keep track of everyone. Children might be separated from their parents. Linking the passengers was a risk; if the wind shifted, they would all be swept into the open waters of the Chesapeake. He took the gamble.

Meckling sent Steve to fetch a couple of long lines and headed into the lounge. He didn't take a head count as he passed the line through the lifejacket straps of Nancy Madden's life jacket. If he had, he would've noticed that two people were already missing. Perry Schwartz and Charles Savoy had climbed to the deck and jumped over moments before.

As the line threaded, Girlie Chesson, who was a Red Cross nurse with training in water survival, snipped the legs from the men's pants so they would be less encumbered. John Ferguson and his father were the next in line to get roped together. John Junior looked for Debbie Killip. Killip, who was traveling alone, had enjoyed the Fergusons' company. They had chatted pleasantly over breakfast that morning as the winds built and the boat seemed to be hurrying across the Bay. They had shared a sense of exhilaration as the boat traveled so quickly for the first time.

Now, John looked at the deck, awash with waves and knew the ship was going down.

The wave that dealt the fatal blow to *Marvel* hit the ship broadside. This time, the ship did not recover. Too much water had poured into the hull, so it lay on its side for a long moment as if giving up. The company assembling on the fantail and in the deckhouse had not finished passing the line through their lifejackets when they were inundated.

On the Beach

Just to the south of Herring Bay, the towns of Chesapeake Beach, and its smaller neighbor, North Beach, Maryland, have the scruffy charm of faded beach resorts. The Bayfront "Beaches" were a major summertime destination for Washingtonians from 1900 until 1952, when motoring vacationers could conveniently reach the Atlantic seaside via the newly opened single-span Bay Bridge near Annapolis.

Otto Mears, a railroad magnate, developed Chesapeake Beach at the turn of the 20th century. His vision was a Chesapeake version of Atlantic City, the glamorous resort 200 miles north on the New Jersey shore. He built a boardwalk promenade, a casino, bath house and several restaurants, bringing the excitement of a seashore destination to southern Maryland. During the early 1900s, a roundtrip train ticket from Washington to Chesapeake Beach cost a quarter and took an hour. Steamboats from Baltimore docked on weekends along the quarter-mile pier.

The Depression combined with the novel experience of automobile travel to put an end to the day-tripping rail travelers. The last train left Chesapeake Beach in 1935. But both the towns of Chesapeake and North Beach continued to be popular resort destinations. One reason was that outside of Nevada, this part of Maryland was the only place in America where slot machines paid out in cash to casual gamblers. The restaurants along the waterfront had penny, nickel and dime slots until Maryland voters made any gaming illegal in 1967. Gradually, the towns shifted away from their seasonal trade and became year-round communities with just a few echoes of their more vibrant past. But in 1955, the summer crowds still came to the Beaches, by car now, to try their luck at the slots, go fishing on a charter boat or just play on the beach.

During the halcyon days of Chesapeake Beach, when the train was running to Washington, George Weems, a Baltimore steamboat operator, had a vision of his own. He built a long pier into Herring Bay in a tiny harbor north of the more built-up beaches. Here, he built the Fairhaven Hotel, and passengers from Baltimore took the steamboat to play on the peaceful sandstone beaches and cliffs. The hotel had long closed in 1955, but the cottages that many had built there were still popular retreats from the hot and humid city in the summer.

It was here in Herring Bay, just off Fairhaven, north of Chesapeake and North Beach, that Meckling sought to ride out the storm with *Marvel*. The big ship was a frequent visitor in calmer weather. People in the cottages sometimes heard music from *Marvel* on quiet summer evenings. Some young residents would row out to the ship which could anchor as close as a few hundred yards from shore. This was a spot both Meckling and Steve MacDougall knew well.

In the protection of a rock jetty on one side, and a shoal, they thought, incorrectly, that the wave action might be mitigated. Instead, they found themselves at the mercy of the northeast wind. With no other choice, they anchored behind the shoal and hoped that the wind would shift.

Out of the Water

That stormy August 12, the Kvale family was hunkered down in their waterside cottage in a summer community called North Beach Park. The huge waves crashing on the beach and stone jetty brought the two grown Kvale brothers outside for a look just before 6pm. What they saw as they stood out front of their home was hard to believe. A woman seemed to emerge from the mist and waves. No mirage, the woman was Deborah Killip, the first survivor to make it to shore from *Marvel*.

The brothers rushed into the water and carried her into the house. Though drenched and exhausted, she was able to tell the family that *Marvel* had broken up nearby. Twenty-seven people were struggling for their lives in the churning waters. Listening, Edwina Cox, mother-in-law to one of the brothers, picked up the telephone.

Cox's calls triggered an extraordinary response from the State Police, Coast Guard and the neighbors who sprang into action and launched a rescue operation in a matter of minutes. People drove to the beach to help. State Police ordered the North Beach Volunteer Fire Department to mobilize all men and declared the station as headquarters for the response. The call went out to surrounding jurisdictions, and soon the operation was in full swing. Ambulances, lights flashing, lined up along the beaches to get aid to the injured. Locals gathered along the jetty to look out for the survivors. They formed a human chain in the stinging wind and waves, hoping to keep survivors from being bashed against the rocks. By this time, around 5:30 in the afternoon, the phone lines were down. Left wondering what was going on, more people made their way to the beach.

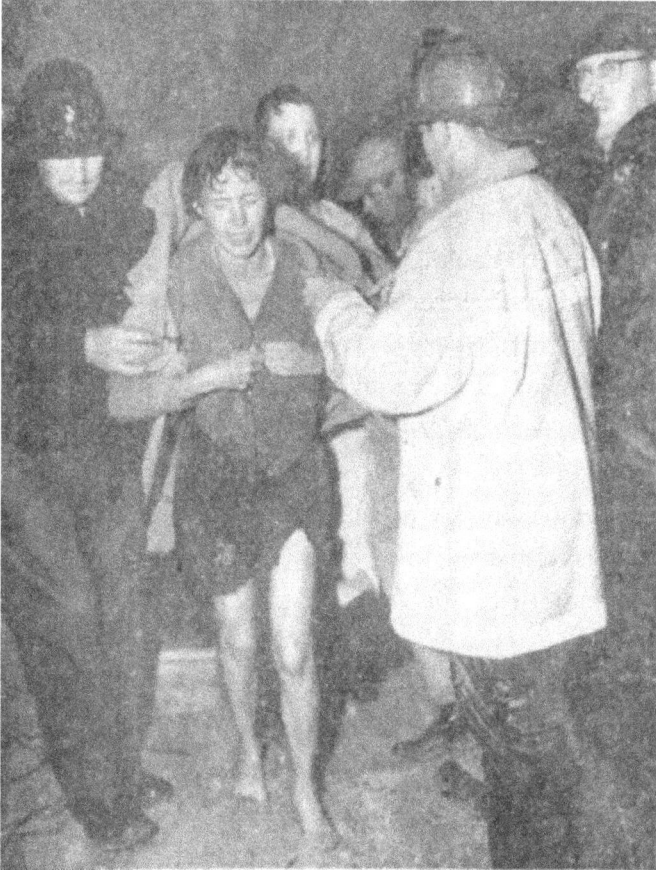

BAY SURVIVOR—North Beach—One of the 13 survivors of the cruise ship sinking in Chesapeake Bay, anguish of the ordeal etched on her face, is helped ashore by firemen and volunteers.

Lives Lost and Saved

Swept off the deck, young Ferguson surfaced in a chaos of foaming water not far from his father. The line Meckling had hoped would keep his passengers together was entangling him, hampering his fight for survival. Suddenly he was freed by, he believed, his father's hand. But as he called frantically, the older man slipped away. Trying to understand the disappearance afterward, young John concluded that the heavy wooden spar swinging wildly from the mizzenmast had knocked his father unconscious. John was utterly alone. The spray blowing off the waves created a white curtain that obscured everything around him.

Amid pieces of the breaking-up ship he saw the top of the deck house, where he had enjoyed evening hours in the company of the young adults onboard. It was a large enough piece of flotsam to become his life raft. But it made an unsteady perch, and he kept slipping off until he found a foothold on the edge between the roof where steps had led down to his cabin.

John drifted for the next three and a half hours, struggling to stay with his raft. There was nothing but the water and slashing rain, and he was making little progress in any direction, it seemed. At one point, Hillary Nevin, the youngest passenger, floated face down in the rolling waves. Eventually, he caught glimpses of shore between pitching into the troughs of the waves. Suddenly, the raft scuffed to a stop in the sand. Momentarily confused, John slipped off and realized he could stand. He was still several hundred feet from shore, but he had made it. He wiped his face, found his footing and walked toward the lights of ambulances. He was the second person to reach the beach.

When the deadly wave struck, Steve was the last one to go over. He had made one last pass down below, wading through waist-deep water to be sure no one was left behind.

Meckling, too, was swept into the water. He struggled to find the surface from under one of the sails, fighting for an edge and a breath. He emerged to see Nancy Madden next to him. He grabbed her and the young nurse, Meryle Hutchinson, then deckhand Steve.

The four were holding close when Frances Roberts emerged; they caught her in their desperate embrace. She had been inside the deckhouse when the ship rolled and began to break up. She remembered later thinking, as she fought her way out through a jagged opening, that she had to survive and get home to her little girls. She never saw her husband, Bert, alive again. She later concluded that, acting on his doctor's instinct to assist passengers, he waited too long to make his own escape, perhaps saving another's life. His body was recovered with a large gash in his head; Frances suspected he was hit by debris.

The shoreline was barely visible. The group stayed together, arms linked when possible, riding the huge waves. Meckling called for them to hold their breath as the sea washed over, keeping a sharp eye on their progress. He knew there was a real danger of missing the shore and floating back out into the open water. They bobbed in the dashing waters for hours, making little headway.

Eventually, a wooden duck blind swaying on narrow poles appeared in the distance. It was a meager shelter, but they made for it. The five made their way toward it as best they could, working against an ebbing tide. Perry Schwartz had made it to the blind just minutes earlier. He called out so they could keep their course toward him.

The duck blind was a typical makeshift affair, common on the Bay, built to conceal hunters as flocks of ducks mistook the brush-covered structure for a tree. The platform, usually no larger than 20 feet square, is made by driving poles into the shallow bottom, then topped with a simple treehouse-style shelter. During the season for goose and duck, hunters came to the blind in small skiffs, then climbed a ladder onto the camouflaged platform.

This particular duck blind was a welcome respite from the waves and stinging rain that assaulted the skin like needles. The castaways clambered up the ladder and huddled together, growing cold in the wind. When Nancy Madden saw the lights of the emergency vehicles on the beach, she waved wildly with the yellow rain hat that she had retrieved from her cabin during the hectic last moments on the ship. She had risked wading through thigh-deep water for this very reason. The bright-brimmed hat shone like a beacon. Her forethought to retrieve it might have saved those six lives.

What happened next was nothing less than heroic.

When Madden's sou'wester was spotted, the excitement on the beach was electric. Several fishing boats set out toward the blind only to turn back when they bottomed out in the shallows. Nearby neighbors offered their smaller 14-foot skiff with a small outboard to the effort. But it took two brave locals to execute the tricky rescue.

Billy MacWilliams and George Kellum were best friends. World War II veterans who came home to the quiet routines of their Southern Maryland childhood, they served as volunteer firefighters alongside their neighbors. Now they rushed to the beach.

They launched the low-powered skiff into waves that were now breaking over their heads. Every shred of their experience growing up crabbing and around boats came into play as they maneuvered into the seas. Kellum kept his eyes fixed on the blind, pointing the course to MacWilliams, who steered a zig-zag course to avoid flipping the boat. They fought their way to the makeshift shelter, where six shivering survivors awaited rescue. The tiny boat had room for no more than one or two passengers at a time, so MacWilliams called for the weakest to come first. Steve MacDougall was shivering uncontrollably

HUMAN CHAIN formed along jetty at North Beach, Md., removed survivors and bodies cast up by waves. Thirteen persons were rescued from wreck of pleasure cruiser Levin J. Marvel after it capsized, broke up.

at this point. He weighed just 117 pounds that summer and had been awake and working nonstop for 30 hours at this point. Exhaustion and hypothermia threatened him now. He and Meryle Hutchinson were the first to leave the blind. The rest watched and waited as their comrades were ferried ashore. Water was filling the tiny craft. Steve joined MacWilliams and Kellum in bailing furiously.

When the boat neared the beach, a human chain formed to haul each load of passengers from the skiff. It was an efficient and quick rescue. Later, MacWilliams said they were worried there was not enough gas in the boat to make the three trips out to the blind, and there was little or no time to bail the water between trips. The last one ashore was Meckling. Minutes after the captain jumped onto the skiff, the blind was overcome by the waves and broke to pieces.

MacWilliams and Kellam's bravery that day saved six lives. They received commendations from Coast Guard and national fire-fighters organizations. They also received the Bronze Medal for Heroism from the Carnegie Fund. Nancy Madden wrote the nomination letter a week after her rescue. "I sincerely believe their courage merits highest recognition," she wrote, "We were sure the duck blind could not last long. But we did not think anyone could possibly reach us in time."

Reunions

After his rescue, crewman Steve MacDougall was reunited with his friend and fellow deckhand Bill Verge. Bill had skipped the trip in favor of a meeting the young men hoped would make them owners of *Marvel*. The two highschoolers last saw each other the Monday morning the ship sailed. With the new deckhand fired, Verge had come to the dock to help get the passengers settled and *Marvel* out into the Bay.

Both Steve and Bill were apprehensive that morning. Hurricane warnings were posted up and down the coast, but the track of the storm was unknown. Bill watched *Marvel* as it sailed away. He had an uneasy intuition that perhaps he would not see *Marvel* again. At the time, he chalked up the feeling to excitement and anxiety about the upcoming meetings. While Steve sailed off on *Marvel*, Bill remained in Annapolis to see to their futures.

Now it seemed his premonition was coming true.

Friday's weather had deteriorated steadily as the storm approached. Late that afternoon, Bill happened upon a Coast Guard Auxiliary member who often chatted up the crew from *Marvel* and kept his own boat on City Dock. Steve climbed aboard to listen to the marine weather forecast. Instead he heard news that caught his breath in his throat.

"You heard what happened, right? *Marvel* went down," the auxiliary Coast Guardsman said.

Bill raced home to tune in the radio report from WNAV. The local station verified the unthinkable. *Marvel* was lost.

Bill threw himself into his car and took off for North Beach, some 30 miles south. Through slashing rain, he drove south on unfamiliar, winding country roads. Trying to follow the map and watch the road, his mind raced. What had happened? He had to find Steve.

When Bill arrived in North Beach as the dark sky turned toward night, the scene unfolding was surreal. Fire trucks and ambulances from at least five jurisdictions, lights flashing, clustered on the waterfront near the fire station. Rushing into the station to find his friend, Bill saw bodies, covered with blankets and tarps, laid on the floor. Steve was not among them.

Survivors had been taken to the closest hospital, Calvert Memorial, 13 miles away in Prince Frederick, one fireman said. Then another said that Steve and the captain had been taken to Annapolis Emergency Hospital. Bill retraced the drive he had just made, thinking only of getting to the hospital to be by his friend's side.

Steve's stay in the hospital had been short. The resilient teen had recovered from the shivers and wanted to get some food and a bed. Hospital staff wanted to observe him overnight, but he insisted on being discharged. His first stop was across the street from the apartment at G&J Diner, where the boys ate most weekend meals. He appeared in his work clothes, now dry but worse for the wear, his hair matted. The cashier thought she was seeing a ghost. She knew about the shipwreck and hugged Steve before settling him with a cheeseburger. When Bill tracked Steve down, he was telling his story to a newspaper reporter. After a filling meal, Steve went to bed for a 12-hour sleep.

John Ferguson was taken to Calvert Memorial Hospital; he was once again alone. The very best vacation, an adventure in the company of strangers who became friends, had ended with him contemplating the unthinkable loss of his father as he waited for his sister to drive from New Jersey to bring him back home.

SAFE AT LAST—Stephen Morton, 18, of Annapolis, who made his way to a duck blind after the vessel broke apart in one of Hurricane Connie's gales, finds helping hands on the shore.

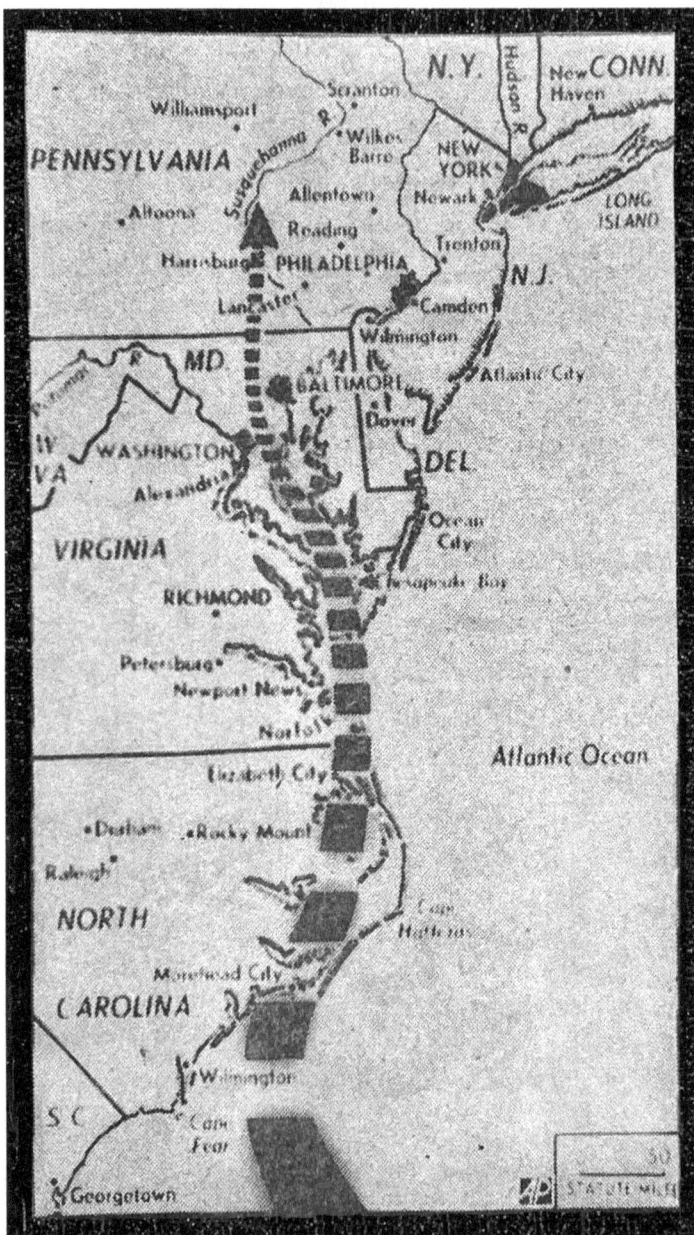

CHAPTER TEN

In Connie's Wake

Marvel was not the only ship to lose its battle with the storm winds on Friday, August 12. *LaForrest L Simmons* came to her harrowing end just an hour before *Marvel* sank. That 88-foot wooden freighter, a schooner converted to diesel, was underway from Baltimore, racing the weather to the less exposed waters of the Choptank. The ship was headed to the State Roads depot near Cambridge, loaded with slag, a byproduct of steel making, that is used to fill potholes. She did not make it past the Sharps Island Lighthouse, marking the mouth of the river. Heavy waves drove the *Simmons* into the shallow water near the light and she foundered there. The captain and the single crewman climbed into a 12-foot rowboat to escape. They spent eight hours tossed by wind and waves, trying to keep the tiny craft afloat. The pair finally washed up on the opposite side of the Bay. The ship sank with its $50,000 cargo.

From North Carolina to New York and beyond, the effects of Connie were deadly. The storm caused a six-foot storm surge when it slammed ashore near Fort Macon, North Carolina as a Category 3 hurricane. Just a year after Hurricane Hazel tore up piers and destroyed homes in the region, Connie took a similar path. Connie impacted all the major population centers of the East Coast, starting in Richmond, Virginia then hitting Washington, D.C., Baltimore and Philadelphia and New York City.

Track of Hurricane Connie

Along the Atlantic seashore, the weekend of August 12 was a washout. The mayor of Ocean City, Maryland, had minimized the storm warnings on one of the last weekends of the resort's season. It is rumored that it was by his intervention with the National Weather Service that hurricane warnings were lowered that beautiful Thursday afternoon.

By Friday, vacationers would have endured lashing rain, high surf and 70 mph winds if they ventured to the beach. A freak waterspout turned into a twister and flattened a beach cottage in Bethany Beach, Delaware, tearing the roofs off many others. The Jersey Shore saw much the same, as a storm surge shoved boats far from the waterways onto dry land and flooded whole communities. Rushing water filled Manhattan's streets and subway tunnels. The metropolis ground to a literal standstill. A record rainfall of 24 inches was recorded at Fort Schuyler in the Bronx. The last remnants of Connie dumped rain on Ontario, Canada, as it dissipated within a cold front over Lake Huron on Sunday night.

In the end, Connie was blamed for 77 deaths and $86 million in damage. The storm left 300,000 in the dark in North Carolina alone. The National Hurricane Center retired the name Connie from its list of storm names. This is only done when a storm is so deadly or destructive that it would be insensitive to reuse the name.

Connie then had an equally devastating successor. Just five days after Connie came ashore, saturating the ground with record rainfall, Hurricane Diane followed a very similar track, causing intense flooding throughout the Mid-Atlantic.

The Human Cost

On Herring Bay, Navy and Coast Guard responders continued searching for the missing all weekend. The last victim was found on Monday, August 15. Wreckage from *Marvel* was washing up on the beaches over several miles during that weekend. Clothing and tins of food mingled with splintered wood. A bright blue book was picked up by a Maryland State Police officer. It was John Ferguson's diary. His name and address were neatly written on the back page. The officer dried the book and put it in a plastic bag before mailing the only record of the voyage back to John. Part of the rigging, attached to two of the masts, floated into the Bay and was picked up later by Eastern Shore watermen. Navy divers came from their station in Annapolis to explore the wreck, whose hull sat on the bottom of Herring Bay in 27 feet of water. They swam the length of the ship and recovered pieces that would next be seen as evidence in Federal Court.

John Ferguson's diary was returned to him
after washing up on shore with debris from *Levin J Marvel.*

Survivors made their way back to their homes. Some
had suffered hypothermia from the long exposure in the
water. Others had deep cuts from their escape from the
lounge when the ship heeled to one side, tipping furniture
and bookcases and tearing the lumber apart. All were
marked in one way or another by the disaster they had
lived through.

Deborah Killip, who had been the first to make it to
shore and raise the alarm, returned to her parents' home
in Rochester, New York. The 26-year-old skier and
sportswoman spoke fully to her local newspaper about
her ordeal. After several hours in the water, shivering
and exhausted, she considered that she might not make
it to shore. To her great relief, she spotted the duck blind

where others would shelter later and knew she had to be close to the beach. Then she saw the shore and the Kvale brothers, who assisted her to their beachfront cottage. Back in Rochester, her grief led her to write letters to the families of the dead. She explained that on a cruise like this, "People get to know one another and become great friends right away." She wrote to John Ferguson, wishing him a smooth start to the new school year, leaving unspoken, but silently conveying, her sense of empathy as another coping with trauma.

In Manhattan, the Sobels' daughter, Phyllis Epstein, was eight months pregnant with her first child and faced with a dreadful dilemma on top of her grief. Her parents were observant Jews, somehow managing to keep kosher on *Marvel* amidst Pinky's Chesapeake and Southern cuisine. Her father's body washed ashore that first night. But her mother remained missing. Should she follow her religious edicts and bury her father immediately? Or should she wait so the couple, who were close in life, could be together in death? She decided to wait for her mother to bury her father. Her mother's body was found on Sunday, with the wreckage. After her brother identified the bodies, they planned a joint memorial for their parents, Louis and Minna. The *New York Times* reported that over 1,000 people attended the service the next week.

Now widowed, Frances Roberts was driven by her brother-in-law to the home she and Bert had lived in just for a few months in New Haven. She packed up a few things, picked up her daughters and went home to her parents' house in East Hartford. It was a difficult adjustment for the family. The introduction of a toddler and a baby into the routines of Frances' older parents added stress to the trauma of the loss of Bert. But Frances could not go back to New Haven. Instead, she bought a home for her girls and herself near her parents and began a long and distinguished career with the state of Connecticut. Her personal experience as a single mother made her an especially appropriate choice for the first director of child day care for the state. Her entire career was a tribute to the lost father of her girls, as she advocated for children.

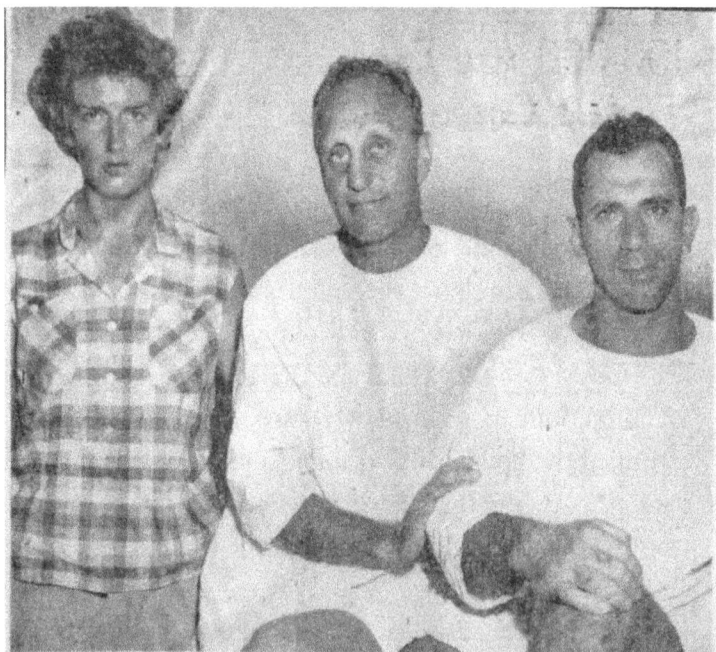

SCHOONER SURVIVORS REST IN HOSPITAL—Prince Frederick, Md.—Three of the survivors of the cruise ship Levin J. Marvel are shown in the hospital here recovering from the harrowing wreck. They are Miss Deborah Killip, 26, copy-writer for a Rochester (N. Y.) advertising firm; Harry Nathanson (center) 48, a physical education teacher from Lawrenceville, N. Y., and Charles Greenwald, 36, a Brooklyn (N. Y.) engineer—Star Staff Photo.

Newspapers across the country picked up the horrifying story of *Marvel*. A decrepit boat capsized, tossing passengers into the surging waters of Chesapeake Bay, with no life raft. Survivors struggled for hours before making it to shore. Fourteen drowned or were dashed upon the rock jetty as they were swept by the seas. One entire family died on their vacation. Dr. Hillard Nevin, a dentist from New York City, along with his wife and son, Hillard, 13, and daughter, Hillary, 9, were among the dead. A photo accompanying the story shows their car, left in Annapolis, with a teddy bear sitting on the rear dashboard, abandoned. The Chessons, of North Carolina, the brilliant doctor from Yale, a brother and sister from Brooklyn, all having a swim together on Thursday—and gone on Friday. What was the captain thinking, taking an old, rotten ship out into a hurricane? The Coast Guard commandant ordered a Marine Investigation into the foundering of *Levin J Marvel* with loss of life.

Meckling himself was devastated. He had lost his ship, the lives of the passengers whom he had tried with all his resources to keep safe, and now he was being pilloried in the press.

Immediately the press began a campaign vilifying Meckling. The narrative evolved that Meckling, a Pennsylvanian who had served in the Coast Guard in World War II, had little sea-time and little exposure to water activities, He was an inexperienced sailor who couldn't even swim. He had no business taking passengers for hire and demonstrated his ignorance by sailing into the teeth of a hurricane. Little was said of his attempts to save his passengers.

Skipper To Be Prosecuted In Wreck Of Bay Schooner

· BALTIMORE—⚓—The Justice Department has been asked by the Coast Guard to prosecute the captain of the pleasure schooner Levin J. Marvel which broke up in Chesapeake Bay with a loss of 14 lives.

The skipper was John H. Meckling of Annapolis, Md.

Meckling said last night he would have no comment on the Coast Guard investigation board's findings until he had examined them.

trade, carried persons exceeding allowances under the law.

2. Failed to maintain proper

Culpability

The Coast Guard convened a hearing in the Customs House in downtown Baltimore just 10 days after the sinking. Initially, the hearing was scheduled for August 19, one week, to the day, after the sinking, but Hurricane Diane was causing more disasters and the investigators postponed until Monday, August 22.

The investigation team included Captain Kabernagel and three other uniformed Coast Guard officers. Their task was to find out exactly what happened, present Facts and Findings, and make recommendations. Over three days, they took turns questioning Meckling, his crew, the shipyard manager, and survivors. John Evans, the silent partner in the cruise operation, did not testify; the Coast Guard was unable to locate him. Coming forward to the defense of Meckling and the boat was Edward Springarn, a professor from Brooklyn, New York, who had enjoyed two consecutive one-week cruises aboard *Marvel* that summer and testified to its soundness and Meckling's ability as a skipper. James Langrall, the assistant prosecutor who would later lead the government case against Meckling, attended each day and took copious notes.

On the first day of the investigation, Meckling gave his first public explanation of the events. He explained that he was aware of the hurricane and followed the storm warnings but was under the impression, from weather reports, it was several days out. He had first thought to ride it out in Oxford but decided the dock there was not secure enough for the large *Marvel*. So he took off for Cambridge, well up in the Choptank River. The party spent Wednesday night there. On Thursday, Meckling decided to start for Annapolis. The weather was fair, and the hurricane warnings had been lowered.

Kabernagel and the others grilled Meckling, who kept his maddening cool during questioning. He deflected questions about his expertise. He pontificated on the care of wooden boats. He tossed off his answers with explanations so lengthy that more than once investigators curtly asked him to keep it brief with just a yes or no answer.

Young Steve MacDougall was also grilled by the panel. He politely responded to question after question about the ship, the yawl boat, the sails and how each emergency was addressed. His story emerged in his answers.

He and Meckling had been up all night when the wind started to howl. Their loss of the sails in the early morning left them in the shipping channel with no means of steering the ship except with the smallest staysail on the bow and the furthest aft mizzen sail, or "spanker," as he called it. The board probed Steve on why they chose to anchor in

Herring Bay. It was, after all, the worst choice from the perspective of the wind. The northeast wind was blowing directly at them there. To the incredulous question, "You chose to anchor on the lee shore?", the shore toward which the wind was blowing, Steve responded, "It was the only thing to do, at certain times a situation presents itself that is not the best, but you must make the best you can of it." That gently delivered understatement encapsulates the education of Steve MacDougall.

Capt. John Mechling, skipper of the ill-fated schooner Levin J. Marvel, takes the witness stand at a Coast Guard hearing to testify concerning the capsizing which cost fourteen lives

It took several months for the board to assemble its findings. In January of 1956, the damning report was issued. The responsibility for the sinking of *Marvel* and the loss of the passengers was laid at Meckling's feet in black and white. Yet the Coast Guard tribunal, with its limited jurisdiction over *Marvel*, could cite him for only three minor violations that seem trivial in view of the events: not keeping a proper lookout, not having a licensed motor boatman to operate the yawl boat, and—in a holdover from World War II—not having port security cards for the crew.

Recommending further investigation, the Coast Guard forwarded the 300-page transcript of the hearing with its findings to the Justice Department. This report would become the basis for the government's case against Meckling and information for Capitol Hill legislators who were preparing to hold hearings of their own. A grand jury was empaneled in late January.

On February 7, the grand jury returned a two-count indictment against John Meckling. He was charged with "misconduct, negligence and inattention to duties," as master of a ship. Additionally, he was charged with "operating the vessel in a reckless or negligent manner so as to endanger the lives and property of the passengers." The charges amounted to manslaughter and carried a potential sentence of eleven years in prison plus fines.

The indictment also was noteworthy for its detail of a shocking list of elements that contributed to *Marvel's* unseaworthiness: "lack of bilge pumps, an operable radio and extensive rot." The grand jury further recommended that vessels such as *Marvel* be required to undergo regular inspections.

The indictment struck one more blow to Meckling.

Part Three:

THE TRIAL

CHAPTER ELEVEN

The Dedicated Lawyer and The Judicious Judge

In January of 1956, John Meckling took a surprise call from Harry Leeward Katz. Katz introduced himself as a Baltimore attorney who had followed the proceedings and the steady stream of negative stories in the press. "They are going to hang you," he said bluntly. "Why don't you come up to my office tomorrow and we can discuss your situation."

Meckling took Bill Verge, who happened to be visiting, with him to visit Katz. The gritty, utilitarian office was in stark contrast to Bill's uncle's plush office. The younger man recalled it looking more like a "gumshoe" detective office, all linoleum and papers. The space reflected the lawyer's no-nonsense approach to the case.

Katz would represent him under one condition: He would abide no second-guessing or interference. Knowing it would be a high-profile case, Katz would work pro bono. Perhaps he also had scores of his own to settle in the courthouse.

Broke at this point, Meckling was relieved that Katz was offering to work without pay. He had no problem letting Katz take command and gladly accepted his offer. This was a smarter move than either Meckling or Bill realized. Despite his unpretentious office, Harry Leeward Katz was no small-time lawyer looking to make a splash. Katz was an old-school courtroom lawyer with deep roots in the Maryland Republican Party and experience on both sides of the bench. Providing equal justice to all was his life-long commitment. He would prove to be a formidable advocate for the defense of John Meckling.

Harry Katz had begun rocking the Maryland Republican party's boat in 1936. As executive director of the Federation of Young Republicans, he openly accused the administration of the Republican governor Harry Nice of corruption. Not at a cocktail party, not in private, but in a speech, he asserted that he knew that the post of Baltimore City Police Commissioner had been offered to an unnamed donor for $10,000. The governor denied the charge and threatened to begin an investigation that could lead to disciplinary action from the Maryland Bar Association against the young attorney.

Katz was undaunted. "I do not propose to be browbeaten by politicians trying to break up a crusade for cleaner and better government," he said.

Katz practiced law in Baltimore, settling estates and writing contracts, but continued his work in government. He was an influential Republican who helped draft the state party's platform in several elections and served on several commissions. In 1953, he was named to the traffic court as a magistrate. In a court well-stocked with political cronies, Katz acted as an unofficial and unwanted ombudsman. He refused to accept the practice of excusing some because of their connections. He also successfully changed the policy of putting teenage traffic offenders in the Baltimore City Jail to await trial. He declared the practice "endangering," to the youths' morals. Instead, they were sent to reform school. But his outspoken accusations of corruption cost him on Green Bag Day.

The so-called Green Bag was a list of appointments made by the governor to offices across the state. Inclusion on the list was the way governors rewarded loyal foot soldiers and donors. The appointments were generally rubber-stamped by the legislature. Republican governor Thomas McKeldin had evidently had enough of Katz and took him off the list for renewal of his appointment to traffic court.

Infuriated and loudly decrying the efforts to silence his reforms, Katz resigned his post, effective immediately, and walked off the job.

A troublemaker to the powerful, Katz was a hero to reformers. A. Risley Ensor, another traffic court magistrate, wrote after Katz's death that he "detested and vigorously fought the firmly entrenched philosophy that traffic and police magistrates should temper justice with political influence."

Intrigued by the Meckling case, just over a year after Katz returned to private practice, he picked up the phone.

The Judicious Judge

The case was assigned to Judge R. Dorsey Watkins. Katz was pleased with the selection. Watkins, who fifteen years later would be named the chief judge of the United States District Court for Maryland, was known to be fair.

The judge also had a renowned intellect. A Baltimore native who had graduated from Johns Hopkins University in 1923, he continued graduate studies in politics and economics, earning a doctorate in 1925. Meanwhile, he was attending law school at the University of Maryland at night. He graduated with what were rumored to be the highest marks in the history of the law school in 1925.

Watkins' dedication to the law was all consuming. He practiced with one of Baltimore's most prestigious firms and lectured the night school law students at his alma maters, both Hopkins and the University of Maryland. His colleagues marveled at both his razor-sharp mind and his common sense. Mild and gently humorous, Watkins seemed the perfect type of judge.

August 12, 1955 was a historic day for Watkins as well as for Meckling. The very day that Meckling was struggling to save his ship and passengers, Watkins was appointed by President Dwight D. Eisenhower to fill a vacancy on the Federal District bench in Maryland. It was the beginning of a three-decade tenure. In March of 1956, just before the Meckling trial began, Watkins was confirmed by the Senate Judiciary Committee to a permanent seat on the court.

Later, in 1973, Watkins would preside over the deal that persuaded Spiro Agnew, the sitting vice president of the United States, to resign by dismissing charges of tax evasion.

Meckling came before Watkins at the beginning of the judge's illustrious career as a thoughtful scholar whose opinions were reasoned and moderate.

On February 25, 1956, Meckling entered a plea of not guilty to two charges: Negligence in operation of *Marvel* resulting in 14 deaths and misconduct as a ship's officer. Judge Watkins set a date of March 5 for filing motions.

Katz's first motion was to attempt to change the venue of the trial. Newspapers had prejudiced a Baltimore jury pool, he argued. The sinking continued to make news, with many articles leading with the adjective "decrepit" or noting the age of *Marvel*. He asked to relocate to Western Maryland, far from the Bay. Watkins rejected the change of venue.

Next, Katz had Meckling waive his right to a jury trial. The case would be argued before Watkins as judge and jury. In response, Watkins promised to avoid consuming any of the coverage of the affair and the trial.

The proceedings began in early April with pretrial hearings. Because Watkins' boating experience was limited to a couple of afternoon outings on the Maryland state yacht around Baltimore Harbor, he wanted to familiarize himself with the mechanics of sailing before judging Meckling. Watkins was an eager student, quickly picking up on the fundamentals of how a sailing ship like *Marvel* was operated. This pretrial hearing was beneficial to Meckling's side, Katz thought, because there was sure to be much maritime jargon from the witnesses that might, otherwise, muddy the waters.

Historic
OXFORD
Maryland
Founded 1683

RED
AVON

RIVER

TOWN CREEK

AO Form No. 110 (Rev. 7-59)

SERVE ON ARRIVAL

Subpoena to Testify Before Grand

United States District Court

FOR THE
DISTRICT OF MARYLAND

Marshals No 19

To Mr. Perry L. Schwartz, 15 East 196th Street, New York, New York.
Mr. John G. Ferguson, Jr., 41 Patten Drive, Bloomfield, New Jersey
Mr. Samuel Finkelstein, 26 Williams Street, New York

You are hereby commanded to appear in the United States District Court for the
District of   Maryland   at   Post Office Bldg., Fayette Ste.
Baltimore   Calvert St   in the city of

testify before the Grand Jury

on the   7th   day of   February   1956 at   10   o'clock A. M. to

the United States.

WILFRED W. BUTSCHKY

By _____

R. W. Forsyth

Clerk

Deputy Clerk

Clerk
Seal

on _____

I served it on the

fee for one day's attendance at the mileage al-

Meet and
association of new acquaintance
28 foot schooner cruise Diem I,
keeping alive the romance of by-
summer days on the Chesapeake

If it isn't the
— Mary but
fun a little
but staring
you soon
John

Mrs. W. Forster
57 Bellwell Ave
Bloomfield
New Jersey

Chapter Twelve

Judgment to Be Proved

The United States v Meckling was called to order on April 18, eight months after the August Coast Guard inquiry. Katz was at the defense table with Meckling. John Langrall and Herbert Murray, both assistant U.S. attorneys, led the prosecution. Seated behind the prosecutors was a uniformed Coast Guard officer. Lieutenant Commander Joseph Gonyeau, investigating officer in the sinking of *Marvel*, was acting as consultant to the government lawyers. The press gallery was packed.

Langrall laid out the case in his opening statement: Meckling had deliberately taken an unseaworthy vessel from a safe harbor in Cambridge on August 11. In doing so he was endangering the lives of the passengers and crew. The captain acted negligently in ignoring storm warnings, not carrying a barometer, not having a radio capable of transmitting, not having functioning portholes to keep out water and not having proper lifesaving equipment or sufficient bilge pumps. It was a sobering assessment delivered in clipped matter-of-fact statements.

Katz previewed a defense of a captain who was a victim of circumstances far beyond his control. Meckling had followed the weather forecasts and observed the winds before leaving Cambridge. The hurricane warning had been canceled on Thursday, and the forecast called for winds of 25 to 30mph, which would make for ideal sailing conditions for the heavy old ship. Meckling believed, with good reason, *Marvel* would be able to make Annapolis safely. He was listening to the official weather statements. Why should he, a civilian mariner, second-guess the government's meteorologists?

The passengers had a fine Thursday, swimming before they set off down the Choptank River to the Bay. Instead of building, the winds died to a whisper and *Marvel* lost time getting downriver.

But the wind picked up in the morning, with gusts that tore the mainsail from the ship. His only hope was to run across to Herring Bay, where he thought they would ride out the storm. Instead, seas that reached twenty feet overwhelmed the old ship. As *Marvel* went down, Meckling did everything he could to bring the passengers to shore.

As for the litany of malfunctioning equipment, Katz flatly disagreed and promised to show that the radio worked, the bilge pumps were in good nick, the portholes closed properly and, most importantly, the ship was seaworthy. A prospective buyer of the vessel would testify that it had been inspected at the shipyard and found to be sound.

In his opening argument, the prosecution had called the ship "dry rotted, especially above the waterline." The government case relied upon his establishing the unseaworthiness of *Marvel*. Now Langrall intended to prove it.

Witnesses for the Prosecution

The first witness for the prosecution was the manager of Booz Brothers Shipyard in Baltimore, where Meckling had taken *Marvel* in 1954 to caulk the seams and make repairs below the waterline. Elias Barthlow told the judge that Meckling had not wanted to make any more repairs than necessary and was in a rush to get the vessel out of drydock and on vacation cruises.

"Was it safe to take the ship out in the conditions that Meckling had on August 12?" Langrall asked. "No," the shipyard manager responded.

Barthlow had given the same testimony at the earlier Coast Guard inquiry. But this time he was going to have to face cross examination by Harry Katz.

Katz jumped to his feet as he began his cross-examination. His tone was accusatory as he questioned the ship repairer. "So, you would not have taken the ship out in the condition you turned it over to Mr. Meckling in?" Katz demanded.

"No sir."

"Would you have taken passengers on the ship?"

"I would not," Barthlow admitted.

"Yet you took Mr. Meckling's money and sent the ship on its way."

A chastened Barthlow answered, "I did what Mr. Meckling asked me to do."

After Barthlow's challenged testimony, Langrall called a pair of Navy divers to further the argument that *Marvel* was unseaworthy. The two divers who had surveyed the wreck early on Sunday after the storm passed offered almost identical answers to the prosecution's questions, suggesting to Katz they were coached. However, they diverged on critical details.

The first diver claimed that he had swum the length of the ship, then walked along the decking and noticed significant rot. The second diver said the deck had been washed away. With the crowbar he was carrying, he had easily pulled boards off the hull. He then claimed to have been able to pull a porthole free and swim it up to the surface to be entered as evidence.

This time, Judge Watkins questioned the divers in a cross-examination that discredited both witnesses. The judge said, "Wait a minute, your fellow diver told us that the deck was intact, and he was able to walk along it, and you say it was torn off?"

The diver responded in respectful but succinct military style, "Yes, sir, it was torn off."

"And you are telling me you had a crowbar but did not use it to dislodge this porthole?" the judge asked.

"Yes, sir."

"And then you were able to carry both of these to the surface?"

"Yes, sir," the diver answered.

"Well, now that is some impressive swimming," Watkins replied. After the damage done by the judge's questions, Katz let the witness go without questioning him further. The Navy divers' obviously coached testimony and the presence of the Coast Guard investigator advising the prosecutors added up for Katz. Clearly, he realized, this trial was about more than Meckling's guilt or innocence. For the Coast Guard, this was the case that would push their passenger safety act over the line. In their enthusiasm to win both victories, the prosecution exaggerated the poor condition of the ship and Meckling's incompetence.

Katz was outraged. The former crusading magistrate who believed that everyone should have an equal shot at a fair trial had seen too many sons of wealthy political donors go unpunished in traffic court. He saw too many young sons of Baltimore's poor go to the city's Dickensian jail. Katz had little appreciation for manipulation of the justice system for any reason, even one he might agree with. Here was a textbook case.

The next witness was the traveling Coast Guard inspector who had come aboard in civilian clothes the day before the last cruise sailed. After the Coast Guardsman had testified that the ship had made its condition known to him on his incognito inspection, Katz wanted to know more about his methods. His cross-examination was another scathing rebuke of authority.

"Did you probe any of the planks or structural members of the ship to check for rot?" Katz asked.

"No, as I said, we were merely looking the ship over," the inspector replied.

"But you were able to ascertain that there were rotting timbers and planks?"

"Why, yes, I already said that," the inspector smartly answered.

Katz then walked back to his table, produced a piece of painted wood and brandished it in front of the inspector.

"Would you say that this is rotted?"

"Of course not," said the inspector, looking puzzled.

When Katz flipped over the plank, it was wormholed and rotten.

Another witness was discredited by his own arrogance.

It is possible Katz had another advantage. Langrall had attended the initial Coast Guard investigation and heard the Coast Guard's arguments. Familiarity might have made him lazy in his preparation of witnesses. Katz, who had not been there, came fresh to the transcript, perhaps finding holes that Langrall had missed.

Next, the scrambling prosecutors called on a weather bureau official to reiterate the dreadful and ample warnings it had issued all week long.

Two survivors then swore that the ship lacked the essential gear that might have saved them. Perry Schwartz, the electrical engineer from New Jersey, testified that the radio was in deplorable condition. The tuning knob was corroded, he said, and wires were "just twisted together." He said he made vain attempts to fix the radio during the period just before the sinking and had no luck; there was no power to the antenna.

John Ferguson was also called by the government lawyers to testify about his ordeal. His description of floating alone in the water for hours brought focus back on the human toll of the tragedy. Ferguson also testified that the yawl boat, which might have been a lifeboat, was in poor condition.

Those two witnesses put new life in the prosecution's case.

Prosecutors wrapped up with Captain William C. McEwen, a retired ship master, as an expert witness. He told the court he held a British Extra Master's Certificate that allowed him to operate any size vessel anywhere in the world. The 70-year old seafarer expounded authoritatively on the necessity of a barometer, which *Marvel* was not carrying. He also was asked to speculate on whether or not Meckling might have made it to Annapolis had he not lost sails. Judge Watkins stopped Langrall from that line of questioning, saying that while he respected the expert witness opinion, he would not let him judge the case at hand.

Harry Katz pounced. He pressed the expert on the importance of understanding local waters when navigating. Then he got him to admit that he "never had the pleasure of sailing in the Chesapeake."

At this discredited point, on April 25, 1956, the prosecution rested its case. Harry Katz had provided a vigorous defense within the first phase of the trial. He had sought to neutralize each one of the witnesses, in turn. It was a tall order: The case against Meckling was strong, making it difficult to not appear to be nit-picking. His decision to forego a jury trial was the correct one. He could now focus on the intelligent judge and provide the doubt that would exonerate his client.

CHAPTER THIRTEEN

The Defense

Katz's defense of Meckling depended on witnesses who could challenge the claim that *Marvel* was unseaworthy. He would subpoena and examine friendly witnesses from crewman Bill Verge to satisfied passengers of earlier cruises to survivors still in mourning to watermen to Coast Guardsmen all the way up to the rank of admiral.

Bill Verge, who had seen a commercial future in *Marvel*, was one of the first to testify—only after Katz had called in political favors. He would be an important witness because he was familiar with the ship both as a crewmember and as a prospective buyer. His youth—he had yet to finish high school—was balanced by his clarity of manner and speech. It didn't hurt that he was the son of a Navy admiral and World War II hero.

By the time of the trial, Verge brought another advantage to Meckling's defense. He was himself a Coast Guardsman. His assignment to the Coast Guard buoy tender, *Jonquil*, based in Norfolk, made him a convenient witness. Indeed, Bill often joined Meckling during the trial preparation. Appearing as a witness, however, would not prove so easy. After the subpoena was issued, Bill was ordered to report to a different ship, this one in the far North Atlantic.

This Coast Guard's maneuver to prevent a uniformed serviceman from testifying for the defense incensed Katz.

He used his influence in Washington to rescind the orders for Bill to leave the area.

On the stand, Verge testified that he had made an underwater inspection of the hull and had visited the shipyard manager at Booz Brothers. The ship was in fair condition, he was told. With some work it could be just fine.

His impressive testimony was set off by his Coast Guard uniform. The prosecution made quick work of its cross-examination to get him off the witness stand.

Next Katz called on a satisfied cruiser. Edward Spingarn, an English professor from Brooklyn, had sailed with Meckling on *Marvel* on one of her first cruises in 1954. He enjoyed his voyage so much that he signed on for a second trip, spending two weeks straight aboard, in all types of weather. Now he testified that the boat was "solid as a rock." When *Marvel* encountered a squall, he said, the large vessel "didn't even rock."

Next, Katz called witnesses to consider how *Marvel's* seaworthiness was affected by its instruments.

The condition of *Marvel's* radio had been criticized by prosecution witnesses. Survivor Perry Schwartz, the electrical engineer, had testified that the radio was in deplorable condition. He said he made vain attempts at repair as the ship flailed in distress.

The allegation didn't gibe with Katz's reading of the earlier Coast Guard examination transcript. There was more to the story, and he was determined to find out what.

Throughout the voyage, passengers had routinely made ship-to-shore calls via the marine operator in Norfolk. That fact suggested that the radio had always been fully operational. Even if the wind had damaged the antennae, a Mayday call had been sent. Someone must have heard the call.

To confirm that suspicion, Katz sent Meckling and Bill Verge to the villages surrounding Herring Bay to do some investigating. Meckling was to ask around at the watering holes frequented by local watermen to see if anyone had received *Marvel's* distress call. They found their witness in Deale, a Herring Bay village a few miles north of the sinking. Just a few inquiries led them to the Marshalls' small boatyard, where young Thomas, who had heard the call that day had not registered its importance. At first, his parents were reluctant to agree to put him on the stand, but they ultimately agreed. He was added as a surprise witness for the defense.

Why had he not come forward before? "I didn't know anyone was looking for me," he said.

Would a barometer have saved *Marvel* and the 14 lost lives? That had been the claim of expert witness for the prosecution Captain William C. McEwen. The 70-year old seafarer expounded authoritatively on the necessity of a barometer, which *Marvel* was not carrying.

Why not? Was its absence simple carelessness on Meckling's part?

In fact, there was a better reason that *Marvel* sailed with no barometer. Previous owner Herman Knust told the judge that *Marvel's* barometer was hanging in his farmhouse in Virginia. He said it was an "oversight" that he did not give the instrument to Meckling when he purchased the ship.

Would the instrument have made a difference? Katz countered the McEwen with his own expert witness, Captain Robert Shores, of Deal Island, Maryland, a remote community on the Chesapeake. McEwen's knowledge spanned the world; Shores was the epitome of "local knowledge." He had worked on *Marvel* for years as a relief captain under Knust and Meckling. He had a half a century of experience in the waters and dozens of trips on *Marvel*.

The old captain proved a credible counterpoint to McEwen. His matter-of-fact statement that he found little use for instruments such as a barometer in the Bay was hard for prosecutor Langress to refute under cross-examination.

Finally, Katz questioned the seaworthiness of the portholes. To break the prosecution's argument that they were rotted, he called on another expert witness, the maid who cleaned *Marvel's* cabins between cruises. She testified that all the portholes operated properly the day before the final voyage.

In dispensing with the prosecution's specific accusations, each in turn, Katz cast doubt on the government's argument that *Marvel* was unseaworthy.

The Stories of Survivors

After many sharp cross-examinations of government witnesses, Katz now needed to show Meckling in a different light. He alleged that faced with a terrible situation, Meckling had made his decisions not in ignorance but in his best hope of saving his passengers. Survivors of that terrible day now helped Katz build his case for Meckling's character and trustworthiness.

Charles Savoy, the ship's steward, testified that when he had gone ashore in Cambridge the morning of August 11, he had not seen the storm warnings flying at the yacht club near where the ship was docked. This was an important point, because, testifying for the prosecution, the yacht club manager said he lowered the hurricane warning flags and replaced them with storm warning flags. Through conflicting testimony about the weather bureau's decision to remove hurricane warnings as Connie's track seemed to veer, Katz was able to cast doubt on the assertion that Meckling had intentionally sailed into the hurricane.

Next up was the ship's cook, Elry Pinkney, perhaps the most engaging witness for the defense.

Pinkney was from a prominent Annapolis family. His forebearers, the founders of the African Methodist Episcopal church downtown, owned a large parcel of waterfront property just to the south. Elry Pinkney had served his country in two wars in the Navy. The local VFW post would later bear his name.

During his service, he had cooked for the likes of Herbert Hoover and other top brass. On *Marvel*, he was

"Pinky," looking out for the young deckhands, cooking up Southern specialties and delighting the New Yorkers with his charm. In a segregated town like Annapolis, he also knew how to play the role of Uncle Remus. That was the character he chose when he took the stand.

Asked to describe the day's events, Pinkney launched into how his menu plan had been disrupted by the weather. He had had to substitute cold sandwiches for lunch for his famous crab cakes. Under questioning from prosecutor Langrall and Judge Watkins, he returned repeatedly to his secret crab cake recipe instead of answering questions specific to *Marvel* and its condition. Asked about the yawl boat, the radio, or the portholes, he always gave a quick and non-committal answer and returned to his crab cakes.

It was maddening to the prosecutors. Finally the gentle Judge Watkins said, "Mr. Pinkney, I am sure you make the very best crab cakes in Maryland and I certainly would love to taste them one day, but can you please answer the question?"

Finally, the prosecution dismissed Pinkney, a knowledgeable witness who had decades of experience on ships, without hearing one piece of evidence that *Marvel* was unseaworthy. As he exited the courtroom, he caught Bill Verge's eye and gave him a wink.

Katz produced another survivor to play counterpoint to John Ferguson's moving testimony for the prosecution. Nancy Madden, the Washington professional and intrepid single traveler, defended Meckling's actions that day. Madden said that she literally owed her life to John

Meckling, "who had done everything humanly possible to save the passengers."

Meckling Testifies in His Own Defense

Climaxing the trial was the testimony of John Meckling. Katz had made the calculated decision to put Meckling on the stand because he was a credible witness as well as an affable character. Now Meckling told his story, that of a man who had lost everything and was facing imprisonment despite making every effort to keep his passengers safe.

Judge Watkins questioned him closely. At one point, he asked, "Forgetting everything that had gone before, was there anything that might have been done to change the situation? When you saw you had to abandon ship, why didn't you dump your anchors and let the ship drift in as close as possible to shore?"

"I could not get to the anchors because the foredeck was under six to eight feet of water," Meckling replied.

Watkins further questioned Meckling on other possible ways he might have saved lives. Why had he not used the yawl boat to ferry people ashore?

Even if it had not been swept away, it would have been of no use in the tremendous seas, Meckling answered.

Katz's calculation was correct: Meckling answered the judge's questions with a mix of respect and clarity that came across as honesty.

Not to Langrall, the government's lead prosecutor. He was not swayed by Meckling.

On cross-examination, he questioned the captain about the ship's massive sails, which only the night before had helped give the ship steerage into safe harbor at Poplar Island. Had the sails been taken down or were they blown off their masts?

Meckling could not summon his usual clarity. At one point he said he had asked for help from passengers to lower the sails; at another he claimed a gust had blown the sail off. In reality, both were correct.

But Langrall closed his prosecution by calling discrepancies between testimonies in the Customs House and in the courtroom a pattern of lies.

Meckling "had most likely lied to the Court," he said.

CHAPTER FOURTEEN

The Coast Guard's Special Agenda

For the Coast Guard, proving the guilt of John Meckling was not only an end but also a means to a larger end. The confrontation he and his unregulated ship had caused with the Coast Guard a year earlier seemed to have opened the door to the service's long desired regulation of small passenger vessels and pleasure boats. Now, that greater purpose gave Katz a surprising defense.

At the time of the *Marvel* tragedy, sailing vessels taking passengers were not regulated or required to be inspected unless they were very large, over 700 gross tons. The Coast Guard had gone to great lengths during its initial August 1955 investigation to try to catch Meckling using the yawl boat as an auxiliary source of propulsion because that use would have made the ship subject to regulations already on the books for power vessels. *Marvel* escaped that trap. Meanwhile, the Coast Guard continued to urge Congress to write regulations into law.

Around the time of the trial, Congress was finally considering two versions of a bill to regulate multiple aspects of recreational boating, including "taking passengers for hire." One of those bills was the brainchild of Representative Herbert Bonner of North Carolina—a state that was home to pirates, countless miles of coastline and inland waterways and, of course, the Graveyard of the Atlantic, Cape Hatteras. For six terms, Bonner had served as the chair of the House Merchant Marine and Fisheries Committee. He had made federal legislation for boating safety a priority during his tenure.

Congressional hearings before the Merchant Marine committee in January included commandant of the Coast Guard Admiral Alfred C. Richmond, who urged the committee to close the loophole that *Marvel* had sailed through. Richmond had used *Marvel* as an example of an "unseaworthy vessel" taking passengers. His statements in congressional testimony had caught Katz's attention.

During that Congressional hearing, the House Committee of Merchant Marine and Fisheries had not only Meckling but also Richmond in the hot seat. A New York congressman had questioned the Coast Guard's response to Meckling's letter following his 1954 run-in with Kabernagel. Richmond had repeated that use of the yawl boat would subject *Marvel* to inspection but use as a sailing vessel would not.

A congressman asked why Richmond did not add that the vessel was unseaworthy. The admiral said the yawl boat played no role in the sinking whereas the unseaworthiness did.

Now, in the Federal courtroom in Baltimore, Katz's plan was to use Richmond's words to secure Meckling's acquittal. The clever lawyer subpoenaed Admiral Richmond for the defense.

Again, the Justice Department and Coast Guard rebuffed the subpoena as a disgrace. Once again, Katz used his Republican connections to get his way. This time, a call from Vice President Richard Nixon compelled Richmond to the stand.

Under oath, Richmond read his testimony from the Congressional Record.

"Any vessel, sound or unsound, would have foundered in the hurricane winds at anchor that day," the admiral read.

Judge Watkins was puzzled. Why, he asked the admiral, had he previously stated that the foundering was caused by the unseaworthiness of the ship? Richmond acknowledged that he had relied upon the Coast Guard investigation's report.

The judge then asked if there could have been a way to save the ship and its passengers that day. Richmond echoed Katz's argument that Meckling really had no choice but to run before the wind. Any boat, he said, whether a power vessel that lost its engine or a vessel under sail, would be in the same situation under the circumstances.

With that, the Coast Guard admiral refuted unseaworthiness as a cause for *Marvel's* sinking.

To further drive home the admiral's point, Katz called Lt. Commander Joseph Gonyeau, an investigating officer from the Coast Guard. Gonyeau had been the most aggressive questioner in the original investigation. Now he sat behind the assistant district attorneys, coaching the prosecution throughout the trial.

Calling Gonyeau to testify on behalf of Meckling was a nervy maneuver by Katz. Gonyeau initially refused, arguing that he did not have permission from his superiors. Judge Watkins called a 30-minute recess and directed Gonyeau to call Admiral Richmond for approval. He did, and was sworn in. Gonyeau gave a new definition to the term "hostile witness."

Katz asked Gonyeau to describe the sinking of *LaForrest L Simmons*, the freighter carrying slag that sank just an hour before *Marvel*. Katz pressed Gonyeau to explain how the captain and his deckhand had been forced to abandon ship and drift for nine hours across the Bay before landing on the western shore. Then, in effect, reiterating Admiral Richmond's testimony, Katz asked about the inspection status of the wooden motorized freighter. It had been fully inspected in 1955, Gonyeau said, and had foundered strictly because of the weather conditions. Katz had found Richmond's "any vessel."

As Katz continued to draw similarities between the freighter and *Marvel*, Gonyeau grew belligerent. He blurted out that Meckling "ought to be in jail!" After his performance, Gonyeau was not seen in the courtroom again.

Further Coast Guard testimony gave the uneasy supposition of railroading greater weight. The Coast Guard had made much of the fact that *Marvel* had never been inspected officially except for the most basic safety inspection. In fact, the Coast Guard had inspected by deception. In a "plainclothes" visit, the traveling inspector and his boss from Washington came aboard as if they were considering a trip. The Coast Guard justified the ruse by claiming it was unable to board the vessel.

By no means, Meckling told Katz. Indeed, the Coast Guard regularly visited the ship in their patrol boats and occasionally boarded. Meckling recalled inviting them to lunch, and the young Coast Guardsmen joined the ship's company for Pinky's delicious meal. Further sleuthing by Katz produced an 8mm home movie of one of the visits. The film-making passenger sent it from her home in New York. Katz succeeded in having it entered into evidence during the trial over the prosecution's objections. The 20-minute home movie clearly showed the patrol boat coming alongside *Marvel* and the crew boarding the vessel, shaking hands all around and chatting with passengers.

Judge and spectators in the darkened courtroom watched the obvious contradiction in silence. The unspoken question: Who was lying about what?

at about 1440 hours EDT on
LEVIN J. MARVEL foun
about 1-1/2 miles
Chesapeake Bay.
were

the Schooner LEVIN J. MARVEL, official number 1955,
a three-masted roundheaded ram-type schooner
length, with wooden hull; of 183 gross tons,
891 and rebuilt in 1919 and 1926.

That the vessel did not have watertight bulkhead
open throughout, with the exception of light
titions separating the various living spaces.

That the vessel was owned by Chesapeake Wind

of 3 State
managing
the compan
owned 31/64
of Phila
pany.

Skipper Is Indicted In 14 Deaths

Grand Jury Cites Ship's Condition In 'Marvel' Sinking; 'Negligence' Charged

BALTIMORE, Feb. 7 (Spl.)
John H. Meckling, skipper of
the schooner Levin J. Marvel
which sank during Hurricane
Connie last August with a
loss of 14 lives, was indicted
on a charge of criminal negligence today.

Staff Photo

JOHN H. MECKLING
. . . faces trial

CHAPTER FIFTEEN

The Verdict

The most important opinion in the courtroom was Judge Watkins'. After closing arguments on May 22, the judge said he did not believe John Meckling had lied. Rather, the captain might have become confused over 14 days of testimony and questioning. Watkins deemed it appropriate to file a written decision on the case. He understood many were waiting for the verdict and promised to return it as soon as possible.

The United States v Meckling, released on June 5, 1956, is an eloquent narrative of the disaster and the events leading up and surrounding the foundering of *Marvel*. The judge explained that there were two charges against Meckling: First, misconduct, negligence and inattention to the duties of the master, causing loss of life. Second, he was charged with operating a vessel in a reckless or negligent manner so as to endanger life.

The first, more serious charge, carried the possibility of huge fines and long prison time. It was also unusually detailed, according to Watkins. It spelled out elements like the lack of a barometer and a functioning radio, leaking portholes, lack of proper lifesaving equipment, for example, as contributing to the deaths of the passengers. The charge consolidated nearly 30 charges referred by the Coast Guard for prosecution by the Justice Department.

Katz had turned the consolidation into opportunity, creating doubt on one after another.

Watkins wrote individually about each: the radio, he concluded, may have worked; but the barometer was not universally accepted as essential equipment. The deciding factor, however, was Admiral Richmond's reluctantly allowed conclusion that "any vessel" would have been in serious trouble in the same circumstances as *Marvel*. Thus, the judge could not "without reasonable doubt" find Meckling guilty of the manslaughter charge. Meckling was visibly relieved on hearing this verdict.

On the other hand, the judge found ample evidence to convict Meckling of negligence. One of the primary elements of this judgment was Meckling's decision to sail short-handed. With another deckhand, the sails might have been switched to gain steerage; the yawl boat motor, which had been submerged, might have been dried out. He also faulted Meckling for failing to continue to broadcast Mayday calls beyond two attempts. Finding Meckling guilty as charged on this count, he sentenced him to one year of jailtime, which he suspended. Watkins also waived the $2,000 fine. He said that Meckling had shown "regret" and was "visibly affected by the knowledge that 14 lives entrusted to him were lost." Watkins also noted the fact that within the testimony of the survivors, "there was not the slightest bitterness."

As the sentence was read, the press thundered out to file their stories. Euretta Meckling sobbed quietly, the stories reported, while John lowered his head into his hands.

Bill Verge stayed with Meckling through the bureaucratic processes that follow a trial and a conviction. They were in the courthouse for several hours before exiting to head back to Annapolis. By the time they descended the granite steps, there was no one on the street. A lone paperboy approached them, offering a copy of the evening paper.

"Meckling guilty of one charge, read all about it."

"This Will Not Happen Again"

Nobody would blame John Ferguson for never setting foot on another schooner after his harrowing experience on *Levin J Marvel*. But, believe it or not, in the summer of 2000, John traveled to the Chesapeake again to take a cruise aboard *Victory Chimes*, *Marvel's* sister ship once known as *Edwin and Maud*. Perhaps, he felt that he needed to complete the voyage he began some 46 years prior.

Between John's trips, much had changed in the world of passenger vessels. He could feel confident that his cruise on *Victory Chimes* would not end up like the *Marvel* voyage. The captain on the ship would hold a Coast Guard Master's license and the crew would be given more than a cursory interview before signing on to work. They would be trained mariners, most working on the ship to gain the required number of hours to advance along their licensing process. Instead of being briefed on where to buy booze, passengers would have had a safety orientation, much like when boarding an airliner.

Victory Chimes was celebrating 100 years afloat when she made the special trip from her homeport in Rockland, Maine, back to Chesapeake Bay. Nevertheless, John found her shipshape. She would have undergone annual inspections and be operating within boundaries set out by Coast Guard's Certificate of Inspection. John

Ferguson could feel safe on *Victory Chimes* because of the regulations that evolved from the foundering of *Levin J Marvel*.

Like other tragedies, *Marvel* was a call to action in Congress.

Before Meckling's trial, Congress was already holding hearings on new, stronger regulations governing small boats. It was at the congressional hearing into *Marvel's* sinking that Coast Guard Commandant A.C. Richmond first made the blame-shifting statement that might have saved Meckling from prison.

Congress also heard from John Meckling. Under questioning by Rep. John Dingell of Michigan, Meckling described the condition of *Marvel* with his usual authoritative cool. He had ordered some repairs, including replacement of rotten planks. He spoke to the conditions of the tragic August day as well. Conditions were so extreme that a converted cargo schooner sank just two hours after *Marvel*. He was referring to *LaForrest L Simmons*.

Not to be intimidated by the congressmen, Meckling ended his testimony with his own advice to the lawmakers. He said that it behooved them, when debating sweeping changes to both vessel inspection and licensing of passenger vessels, to consider the people affected by new licensing requirements. The captains of small passenger vessels, he said, might have little formal education but rich knowledge of the waters in which they operate. They should not be deprived of their livelihood because of "difficult written tests."

Congress moved forward quickly. The House passed its version of the passenger vessel safety bill in February, and the Senate followed suit on April 6 of 1956. President Dwight D. Eisenhower signed the legislation on May 10. Coincidentally, that was the day John Meckling was questioned by Judge Dorsey Watkins.

House Passes Boat Law After Sinking of Marvel

The House passed without objection yesterday a bill stiffening boat inspection laws as a result of the sinking of the sailing vessel Levin J. Marvel off North Beach, Md., in Chesapeake Bay during Hurricane Connie last August.

Fourteen lives were lost in the disaster and the skipper, who survived, is scheduled to stand trial in Federal District Court in Baltimore later this month on charges of criminal negligence. The vessel was exempt from all but cursory inspection because it was a sailing vessel under 700 gross tons.

The measure, which now goes to the Senate for action, would plug this loophole. The bill would require at least every three years inspection and certification of boats carrying more than six passengers in the following classifications: sailing vessels of 700 gross tons or less, barges of 100 gross tons or less and mechanically propelled vessels of 15 gross tons and less. Exempted are public vessels of the United States and of foreign countries.

The measure furthermore prohibits operation of a passenger-carrying vessel until a certificate of inspection has been issued. A fine up to $1000 is provided for each violation.

The measure had the support of the Treasury and Commerce Departments.

In 1958, the Small Passenger Vessel Rule was written into the Federal Register. Rep. Bonner's sweeping Boat Act was also codified that same year. States were given the authority to issue vessel registration numbers to be prominently displayed on all powerboats carrying engines of more than 10hp. Boaters became subject to rules of the road, and captains could be ticketed for speeding and, later, drunken boating. Charter boats like *Pelican* and *Jack* were also affected by the Small Passenger Vessel rule. The old days of the Fisherman's Special, when captains could take as many people who were willing to pay, were ended. Each boat's passenger load was determined by its size. Captains carrying paying customers were required to have a minimum license.

The rules and regulations written mid-20th century might since have deterred captains from taking chances with passengers like Meckling did by leaving Cambridge. Weather forecasting is earlier and much more accurate. But, in the end, it is always the captain who makes the call. Meckling could have waited out the storm tied to the pier in Cambridge. He might have offered bus tickets to passengers who needed to return.

Had he made those choices, Bert Roberts would have returned to his daughters Maggie and Priscilla. The Nevin family would have had a sea story to tell, not a tragedy to mourn. Young John Ferguson might have enjoyed many more adventures with his father. Thousands of opportunities that were missed might have been.

But for whatever reason, hubris or economics, John Meckling did not make those choices. Instead, he took a gamble that turned out to be deadly.

Epilogue

John H. Meckling

After his acquittal, John Meckling created a new life in Louisiana with new wives. Leveraging his mechanical creativity, he patented a new technology for self-contained water systems and founded a company, MHD Systems, to manufacture and install these units. His technology is used worldwide in oil and gas production, airports, and even cruise liners. He died in Louisiana in 2005, at 83, a day before hurricane Katrina ravaged the state.

Stephen Hatfield MacDougall

Steve joined the Coast Guard after surviving the wreck of *Levin J Marvel*. He served on the cutter *Chincoteague* in the North Atlantic. After completing his service, he traveled to Spain, where he met and married Maria Victoria Santiago in 1963. The couple ultimately settled in Miami with their three children, Alexander, Patrick, and Victoria, founding Lysan Forwarding Company. Steve died in 2021.

William Granville Verge

Bill Verge has enjoyed a long and varied career, beginning with four years in the Coast Guard. He next earned a bachelor's degree from University of Miami, where he was accepted without a high school diploma. Four years later, he rejoined the Coast Guard, serving a year in Vietnam and four as commanding officer of the organized reserve training center in Washington, D.C. For four more years he worked for Henry E.I. duPont as president of Sci-Tek, Inc., leaving to form an aviation company, Skyway Aviation. Two years later, he got on his boat and sailed to Florida. He spent 20 years operating, then owning marinas in Melbourne, Florida. Finally he moved to Key West, where he served as a city commissioner. He in now chairman and executive director and founder of the US Coast Guard Cutter *Ingham* Maritime Museum in Key West.

John C. Ferguson Jr.

John's maritime interest continued despite his experience on *Marvel*. After high school, he began a long career at Cunard Line, rising from office boy to cruise staff and traveling to the "edge of everywhere" on Cunard ships. He also worked at the Greek Line and shoreside in luxury cruise sales. He is retired now, living in Tarpon Springs, Florida.

Victory Chimes

Victory Chimes, formerly *Edwin and Maud,* survives her fellow ram schooner *Levin J Marvel* by seven decades and counting. The last of the Chesapeake ram schooners, sails out of Rockland, Maine, thrilling passengers on the windjammer cruises Herman Knust and John Meckling briefly brought to the Chesapeake. She currently awaits another dreamer to take the helm.

Those Who Perished
in the Foundering of *Levin J Marvel*

ANDREW CHESSON AGE: 41 RALEIGH, NC

GIRLIE COMPTON CHESSON AGE: 41 RALEIGH, NC

RHODA FEDDER AGE: 48 NEW YORK, NY

JOHN C. FERGUSON SR. AGE: 62 BLOOMFIELD, NJ

FLORENCE GOLDSTONE AGE: 37 BROOKLYN, NY

WALTER GOLDSTONE AGE: 40 BROOKLYN, NY

HARRY KIRSENER AGE: 58 LAWRENCE, NY

CECILE NEVIN AGE: 40 BROOKLYN, NY

HILLARD R. NEVIN SR. AGE: 42 BROOKLYN, NY

HILLARD R. NEVIN JR. AGE: 13 BROOKLYN, NY

HILLARY CIEL NEVIN AGE: 9 BROOKLYN, NY

BERTRAM H. ROBERTS AGE: 34 NEW HAVEN, CT

LOUIS H. SOBEL AGE: 52 NEW YORK, NY

MINNA SOBEL AGE: 56 NEW YORK, NY

Acknowledgments

This book attempts to tell the story of *Levin J Marvel*, particularly its foundering and aftermath.

It could not have been written without Bill Verge's patient telling and retelling and explaining and retelling again the stories of the schooners and in particular *Levin J Marvel.* John Ferguson was invaluable in sharing his archive, containing his diary as well as his memories of that traumatic day.

Many others have generously shared their knowledge with me, including: Diane Donovan Harrison; Captain Sam Sikkema of *Victory Chimes;* Eric Steinlein, Maggie Roberts Barkin and Priscilla Roberts, Steve MacDougall and his daughter Victoria Miller. Grace Mary Brady of the Bayside History Museum in North Beach shared the archival material they put together when commemorating the 50th anniversary of the disaster.

I apologize in advance if some details are missing or incorrect.

Thanks to Jennifer Bodine, Richard Orban and Brooke Jackson for photography. Thanks also to Sandra Olivetti Martin for her genius editing, Felix Tower for her cheerful assistance and Suzanne Shelden, for her design work.

I also must express my gratitude and love to my entire family who have put up with my stories and supported this project from the get-go. Ditto to all the great friends who must be pretending, at this point, to be interested! Most especially, Jeff Smith, who makes it fun.

PHOTO CREDITS

page vi: Detail of *"Levin J Marvel"* photo by A. Aubrey Bodine.
All Bodine photos are courtesy of A. Aubrey Bodine.com,
copyright Jennifer B. Bodine

page viii: Scanned news clipping: "WRECKAGE OF SMASHED
SCHOONER COMES ASHORE—Chesapeake Beach, Md.—
A piece of the wrecked schooner Levin J Marvel lays on the beach
yesterday, after Hurricane Connie smashed the schooner with wind
and water, killing at least eleven persons. Three more are missing.
Thirteen survivors were pulled from the angry water."
—*Star* Staff Photo. Clipping from John Ferguson Jr.'s scrapbook

page x: Tour map detailing the delights of Chesapeake Windjammer
cruises. Created for Herman Knust's tours by designer Lester Trott.
Courtesy of Bayside History Museum

page xiv: Image of the *Levin J Marvel* and ship's diagram.
Courtesy of Bayside History Archive

page xvi: *Levin J Marvel* sails out of Annapolis Harbor.
Photo by A. Aubrey Bodine

page 2: Herman Knust with his two-ship windjammer fleet c.1950.
Photo by A. Aubrey Bodine

page 4: Souvenir postcard. Courtesy of Grace Mary Brady and
Bayside History Museum *Levin J Marvel* archive

page 7: Skipjack tied up to pier. Digital image by Pat Anderson,
www.shutterstock.com

page 8: *Jennie D Bell* in her working years.
Photo by A. Aubrey Bodine

page 14 and 15: "Cradle of the Deep" image of
Edward R Baird Jr. Photo by A. Aubrey Bodine

page 16: Deep-laden *Edwin and Maude* ready to transport lumber.
Photo by A. Aubrey Bodine

page 18: *Jennie D Bell* languishing in Wicomico River, 1967.
Photo by A. Aubrey Bodine

Deadly Gamble

page 19: Captain Clarence and Mamie Heath on *Jennie D Bell.*
Photo by A. Aubrey Bodine

page 20: *Levin J Marvel* sailing in the Chesapeake.
Photo by A. Aubrey Bodine

page 22: *Levin J Marvel* underway c. 1950.
Photo by A. Aubrey Bodine

page 25: Partial quote: HOPES TO SAIL AGAIN. John Meckling,
owner of the three-masted ram *Levin J Marvel,* shown at wharf in
White Haven alongside an old fish steamer. For the past week "at
Baltimore shipyard...for caulking," Meckling said, "and we should be
in the cruise business by..." Newspapers.com

page 32 and 33: *Pelican* and the Montauk, NY "head boat" fishing
fleet, c. 1949. *Outdoor Life Magazine*

page 36: John Meckling at the helm of *Levin J Marvel,* 1954.
Photo courtesy of Bayside History Archive

page 39: Elry Pinkey. Ship's cook who survived.
Clipping from John Ferguson Jr.'s scrapbook

page 41: *Levin J Marvel* in West River. Souvenir postcard courtesy
of Bayside History Museum collection

page 44: Brochure for Chesapeake Windjammer Cruises, c. 1947,
showing a much more commodious ship than *Marvel* of 1954-55.
Courtesy of Bayside History Archive

page 50: Severn School, junior class, 1955. Courtesy of Bill Verge

page 53: The *Levin J Marvel* spies a freighter.
Photo by A. Aubrey Bodine

page 58: "The Traveling University," a church youth group from
Dayton, Ohio on *Levin J Marvel,* July, 1955. *Star* Staff Photo.
Clipping from John Ferguson Jr.'s scrapbook

page 60 and 61: "Rain over Stormy Sea."
Photo by Elena Schweitzer, www.shutterstock.com

page 62: Vacation Brochure created for Herman Knust's tours
by designer Lester Trott. Courtesy of Bayside History Archive

page 64: Portrait of Minna and Louis Sobel.
Courtesy of Sobel family

page 65: Portrait of Bertram and Frances Roberts.
Courtesy of Roberts family

page 68: News article portrait of Miss Nancy Madden.
Clipping from John Ferguson Jr.'s scrapbook

page 71: News article portrait of John Ferguson Jr.
Clipping from John Ferguson Jr.'s scrapbook

page 77: A close look at the rigging of a Ram Schooner
on a beautiful day. Photo by A. Aubrey Bodine

page 78 and 79: "What a day! Wow!"
Journal entry by John Ferguson Jr.

page 81: Last cruise of the *Levin J Marvel*.
Amity Price Jones map of *Marvel*'s voyage.
Map courtesy of Amity Price Jones

page 93: "BAY SURVIVOR—North Beach—One of 13 survivors
of the cruise ship sinking in Chesapeake Bay, anguish of the ordeal
etched on her face, is helped ashore by firement and volunteers."
Evening Star clipping from John Ferguson Jr.'s scrapbook

page 97: "HUMAN CHAIN formed along jetty at North Beach,
Md. removed survivors and bodies cast up by waves.
Thirteen persons were rescued from wreck of pleasure cruiser
Levin J Marvel after it capsized, broke up."
Evening Star clipping from John Ferguson Jr.'s scrapbook

page 101: "SAFE AT LAST—Stephen Morton, 18, of Annapolis,
who made his way to a duck blind after the vessel broke apart in one
of Hurricane Connie's gales, finds helping hands on the shore."
Evening Star clipping from John Ferguson Jr.'s scrapbook

page 102: Graphic showing track of Hurricane Connie.
Clipping from John Ferguson Jr.'s scrapbook

page 106: Envelope in which John Ferguson's diary was returned
to him—after being found washed up shore with debris from
Levin J Marvel. Envelope photo by Brooke Jackson

page 108: "SCHOONER SURVIVERS REST IN HOSPITAL—
Prince Frederick, Md—Three of the survivors of the cruise ship
Levin J Marvel are shown in the hospital here recovering from the
harrowing wreck. They are Miss Deborah Killip, 26, copywriter for
a Rochester (N.Y.) advertising firm; Harry Nathanson (center) 48,
a physical education teacher from Lawrenceville, N.Y., and Charles
Greenwald, 36, a Brooklyn (N.Y.) engineer." *Star* Staff Photo.
Clipping from John Ferguson Jr.'s scrapbook

page 110: Scanned clipping from a Baltimore Newspaper.
Clippings collage by Brooke Jackson

page 112: "Capt. John Mechling, skipper of the ill-fated schooner
Levin J Marvel, takes the witness stand at a Coast Guard hearing
to testify concerning the capsizing which cost fourteen lives."
Clipping from John Ferguson Jr.'s scrapbook

page 114: Courthouse, Baltimore. Library of Congress, Prints &
Photographs Division, Detroit Publishing Company Collection

page 122: John Ferguson scrapbook photos
from John Ferguson Jr.'s scrapbook

page 131: William Granville Verge. Courtesy of Bill Verge

page 138 and 139: Detail of *Levin J Marvel* from photo
by A. Aubrey Bodine

page 140 and 141: "COAST GUARD BOARD INQUIRING
INTO SINKING OF SCHOONER *MARVEL*.
Members are, left to right, Captains E. H. Thiele, H.C. Moore and
Albert W. Kabermogle. Far right is aide, Lieut. N. N. Gonyeau."
News Post photo

page 146: Collage showing *Washington Evening Star* and other
pieces from John Ferguson Jr.'s scrapbook

page 150: John Ferguson on *Victory Chimes* in 2000.
Courtesy of Janie Meneely

page 153: Scanned clipping of news article from John Ferguson Jr.'s
scrapbook: "House Passes Boat Law After Sinking of *Marvel*."

ABOUT THE AUTHOR

Kathy Bergren Smith is a writer living in Galesville, Maryland. She covered maritime industrial subjects as a photojournalist for 20 years. *Levin J Marvel* foundered just a few miles from her home on Chesapeake Bay.

www.ingramcontent.com/pod-product-compliance
Lightning Source LLC
Chambersburg PA
CBHW022054020426
42335CB00012B/685